Defeat Depression

Understand Your Sadness —and Banish It Forever!

Frank J. Bruno, Ph.D.

Macmillan • USA

Life's Little Keys

Self-Help Strategies for a Happier, Healthier You

ADDITIONAL TITLES

Stop Worrying

Overcome Shyness

Stop Procrastinating

Conquer Loneliness

Get a Good Night's Sleep

To those who struggle
with the problem of depression

Macmillan General Reference
A Simon & Schuster Macmillan Company
1633 Broadway
New York, NY 10019-6785

An Arco Book

ISBN 0-02-861305-8
Library of Congress Catalog Card Number 96-085333

Manufactured in the United States of America
10 9 8 7 6 5 4 3 2 1

Cover design by Kevin Hanek
Book design by Scott Meola

CONTENTS

PREFACE

What *is* depression, anyway?

What are its signs and symptoms?

Is it primarily biochemical in origin?

Or is it caused mainly by psychological factors?

If you are depressed, what can you do about it?

If you want answers to these and similar questions, then this book was written for you.

Defeat Depression explains why people get depressed. And it sets forth practical self-directed strategies for coping with depression.

I believe you will find it to be a helpful, practical book.

ACKNOWLEDGMENTS

A number of people have helped me make *Defeat Depression* a reality. My thanks are expressed to:

Barbara Gilson, senior editor at Macmillan, for her recognition of the value of the book and for being a supportive and creative editor.

Jennifer Perillo, editor at Macmillan, for her assistance and for her appreciation of the book's themes.

George J. McKeon, artist, for his capturing of key ideas in cartoon form.

Bert Holtje, my agent, for encouraging the development of the book.

My wife, Jeanne, for our many meaningful discussions.

My son, Franklin, for our conversations about language and meaning.

George K. Zaharoupoulos, a true teaching colleague, for his steadfast encouragement of my writing projects.

1 A PORTRAIT OF DEPRESSION: THE COMMON COLD OF EMOTIONAL PROBLEMS

If you suffer from either passing depression or chronic depression, you are not alone.

It has been said that depression is the common cold of mental and emotional problems. Most clinical psychologists and psychiatrists talk to one or several depressed persons every day. Expressions such as these are all too frequent:

"Life just doesn't seem worth living any more."

"I don't know why I have to do things. Why do I have to go on? Why do I have to get out of bed in the morning? What's the point?"

"I see flowers and birds and children, but I don't *see* them. I know they're all there and alive. But they seem dull and gray and almost nonexistent to me."

"I seem to be sad and unhappy most of the time. And I don't know what to do about it."

"I've got the blues in the night. And I've got the blues in the day. I never feel like smiling. If I do, it's just to be polite."

And, of course, many people simply say: "I'm depressed."

The opening sentence of this chapter includes the word *suffer*. Depression is associated with suffering.

Depression is a variety of emotional pain. And it is *this*, your suffering, that you want to alleviate.

This book has been written with one primary objective: to be a useful tool that will help you reduce your level of suffering. If you will selectively apply its numerous practical suggestions, keeping in mind your individual personality and needs, you can expect to think and feel better than you presently do.

Principal Characteristics

In one sense it's easy to tell if you're depressed. If you *think* you're depressed, and if you *feel* depressed, then you *are* depressed. Often it's just that simple.

On the other hand, it is actually possible to be depressed and to repress self-awareness by compensating defense mechanisms. In such cases an individual is said to be in a state of *denial*. One example is a manic state in which at the conscious level the individual is full of energy and ready to lick the world. But it is all a type of nervous froth, a kind of psychological whipped cream that will go sour and flat in a short time.

A second example is a person who is manifesting a workaholic syndrome. Compulsive work can be a way of running away from self-knowledge. In short, sometimes before there is consciously experienced depression, there are warning signs and symptoms.

Consequently, it will be of value for you to know what they are. As the chapter title indicates, these signs and symptoms will paint a portrait of depression. And this portrait will help you spot depression in yourself and in others.

Note that in psychiatry and medicine a formal distinction is made between a sign and a symptom. A *sign* is an objective indicator. A *symptom* is an experience. For example, in the case of high blood pressure, an elevated reading on a measuring instrument is a sign. Feeling

uncomfortably hot could be a symptom of high blood pressure. In practice, the academic distinction between a sign and a symptom tends to sometimes blur, particularly in the case of emotional problems. Consequently, the distinction is not particularly stressed in the signs and symptoms that follow. However, it is of some value to have a background knowledge of the difference between the two.

Here are some important signs and symptoms of depression:

1. A general lack of pleasure in life. Familiar challenges, projects, hobbies, or recreations provide no enjoyment. The clinical term used to describe this state of affairs is *anhedonia*. (It is sometimes spelled *ahedonia*; it has the same meaning.)

2. Distortions in eating behavior. We often hear that people overeat when they are depressed. And this can be the case. I think it is true that people often tend to eat compulsively when they are moderately depressed. However, when a person is severely depressed, there tends to be a loss of appetite.

3. Sleep disturbances. Depending on individual differences and various determining factors, some depressed people may find it difficult to sleep. Other depressed people may sleep too much.

4. Disturbances in one's normal activity level. One depressed person may take on a big load or bite off more than he or she can chew in an effort to communicate the idea, "See. I'm not depressed." (Earlier I gave the example of workaholism.) On the other hand, another depressed person may become sluggish and listless.

5. A general lack of energy. The depressed person is prone to say or think, "I'm tired all the time" or "I'm exhausted." It is presumed that the symptom is caused by emotional, not biological factors. However, this can be a fuzzy distinction. Chapter 2 explores the very important subject of the psychobiology of depression.

6. The conviction that one leads a useless, ineffectual life. The individual's own sense of being is devalued. Thoughts such as, "I'm wasting my life" or "I don't amount to much" often prevail.

7. A reduced capacity to think clearly and to solve problems effectively. The person finds it difficult

to focus his or her attention on a subject for a sustained period of time. The common complaint is, "My mind seems to wander."

8. Indirect self-destructive behavior. Examples of indirect self-destructive behavior include the abuse of alcohol, nicotine, narcotics, and other drugs. Compulsive eating, particularly if one has a health problem such as obesity, hypoglycemia, or diabetes, can also be identified as a kind of indirect self-destructive behavior.

9. Preoccupation with thoughts of suicide. (Actual suicide is, of course, *direct* self-destructive behavior.)

Look over the list and make a self-evaluation. There is no hard-and-fast rule. But it is a convention to suggest that if five or more of the signs or symptoms are both present and persistent, then it is quite possible that you *do* suffer from depression.

If you see yourself reflected in the last symptom, preoccupation with thoughts of suicide, it is essential that you seek professional help as quickly as possible. This is a red flag, a psychological warning that must be taken seriously.

In general, if you feel overwhelmed and demoralized by the signs and symptoms of depression, it is prudent to seek the assistance of a clinical psychologist or a psychiatrist.

In order to complete our portrait of depression, let's translate the phrase *common cold of emotional problems* into some statistics. Estimates have varied widely depending on the sample and research methods used by a particular investigator. Nonetheless, it can be stated with some confidence that the figures associated with adults who will suffer significant depression during a lifetime are about 15 percent for women and 8 percent for men. At a given moment in time, about 6 percent of adult women suffer from depression, and about 3 percent of adult men.

Converting percentages into numbers, it can be said that approximately seven million adults in the United States are currently struggling with depression.

Aside from the fact that women are more likely to suffer from depression than men, depression is not associated with other fundamental social factors such as one's cultural background, economic status, level of formal education, or marriage. Depression does not respect *who* you are. The rich and the famous suffer right along with everyone else.

Why are women more likely to bear the burden of depression than men? First of all, let's note that men *do* suffer from depression. The percentages given for men are not insignificant. Both sexes are prone to depression. However, women *are* twice as likely to be its victims.

There have been many attempts to answer the question. One answer has been that women, in terms of cultural training, are more likely to admit that they are depressed. Consequently, they more willingly make appointments with psychologists and psychiatrists. Males tend to see their masculinity threatened when they voluntarily seek counseling and psychotherapy. If this interpretation is correct, then the statement that women are more likely to suffer from depression than men is a statistical artifact, an error based on the way in which data are gathered and reported.

If, on the other hand, percentages are taken at face value, an idea that has frequently been advanced is that some women are dominated and bullied by men. They feel used and abused, and this contributes to a state of depression. The argument is that the traditional woman has been taught to be submissive toward men, to allow the male to be "the king" and "the head of the household." Consequently, there is a loss of self-esteem because the female is treated like a child. Some observers have noted that in many settings, including workplaces,

women often have secondary status. Even if these general explanations are debatable from a broad sociocultural perspective, they can certainly be quite correct in individual cases.

Finally, it has been argued that men are biologically more aggressive than females. As you will see in chapter 3, it is possible that depression is linked in some cases to repressed anger. If men really are more aggressive, they are somewhat less likely to repress anger. If this is the case, then they are in turn less likely to be depressed.

On the whole, gender bias in depression is not of major concern to you. If you are depressed, you are not a statistic. You are one person floating about in the statistical sea. The real issue for you is to *not* be a statistic. You want to look upon yourself not in terms of averages or other people, but in terms of your unique identity and individuality. Depression is a personal problem. And the aim of this book is to help one person cope with depression. And that person is *you*.

The Faces of Depression

Depression can present itself in a variety of guises. There are several related kinds of depression. The principal ones are:

1. Major depressive disorder
2. Dysthymic disorder
3. Bipolar disorder
4. Cyclothymic disorder

Major depressive disorder is very much what it sounds like. The signs and symptoms presented earlier, if severe, tend to be associated with this condition. The individual is very depressed, and there is a real risk of suicide. Significant depression of any kind requires treatment, and this is particularly true of those who suffer from major depressive disorder.

Dysthymic disorder is characterized by a general feeling of sadness and a nagging feeling of being emotionally low. An older term for this disorder was "depressive neurosis." Depression tends to be mild or moderate, and the individual tends to learn to live with it. Also, depression tends to be nagging and persistent, wearing the person down. Dysthymic disorder is common garden-variety depression. And, as already indicated, many, many people suffer from it. As you will learn from this book, it does not have to be endured. Living with chronic depression greatly undercuts the quality of life.

(The word *dysthymic* can be made meaningful by examining its components. *Dys* is a combining form meaning "bad" or "defective." *Thymos* is the Greek word for mood. Consequently the literal meaning of dysthymic is "bad mood.")

Bipolar disorder is characterized by alternating states of mania and depression. An older term for this disorder was "manic-depressive disorder." *Mania* is characterized by great excitement, irrational optimism, unrealistic "big ideas," and excessive activity. Depression has already been described. Although bipolar disorder does contain moments of elation and hope, it is still essentially a kind of depression. The manic phases tend to be brief and the depressive phases tend to be long.

(The term *bipolar* refers to the two poles of a psychological continuum with mania at the "positive" end and depression at the "negative" end.)

Cycloythymic disorder is characterized by periods of hypomania alternating with periods of depression. The combining form *hypo* means "beneath" or "below." Thus, *hypomania* is a term that means "below mania." Consequently, hypomania is a low-grade mania, not as intense as the mania experienced in bipolar disorder. Also, the depression experienced in cyclothymic disorder is not as severe as the depression associated with either major depressive disorder or bipolar disorder. It is correct to look upon cyclothymic disorder as a somewhat less intense kind of bipolar disorder. The mood swings exist, and they *are* distressing. But they are neither as wild nor as erratic as those experienced in connection with bipolar disorder.

(The word *cyclothymic* can be made meaningful by examining its components. The combining form *cyclo* means "circular." As a word in itself, *cycle* means "a recurring period." *Thymos*, you will recall, is the Greek word for mood. Consequently, *cyclothymic* refers to recurring periods of both elevated and depressed mood.)

Although there are four principal clinical terms used to describe the faces of depression, you can see that at root there is, in a sense, only one disorder. That disorder is, of course, depression itself. The four diagnostic categories specify (1) its range of severity and (2) whether or not there is significant mood fluctuation in a specific case.

What This Book Can Do for You

The aim of this book is to help you defeat depression. It will be a helpful companion in the attainment of this important goal in the following ways:

1. Depression will be *explained*. It will cease to be a mystery, a strange something that just happens to you. You will acquire *insight* into why you suffer from depression. Although it is generally asserted by contemporary psychotherapists that the enhanced understanding of the self associated with insight is not a sufficient condition to assure recovery from a personal problem, it is also a common consensus that insight can be very useful. Insight provides a personal gateway into a domain where the self-management of behavior, including its emotional aspects, becomes possible.
2. You will be presented with a number of coping strategies, practical tips, and suggestions that make it possible for you to come to grips with depression and actually *do* something constructive about it. Insight provides the *why* of depression. The coping strategies provide the *how* of better living. This book takes the firm position that depression is, to some extent, linked to negative choices and self-defeating decisions. By replacing these adverse choices and decisions with positive ones, you can make significant personal gains in the overall quality of your life.
3. If you are receiving psychotherapy or taking drugs for depression, this book will help you see that your recovery from depression depends to a large extent on your own thought processes and how

you cooperate with your treatment. A client receiving treatment for an emotional problem is not like a car that is taken to a mechanic. You can't just say to a therapist, "Fix me." You must be an *active* agent, not a passive one, or very little improvement, if any, will take place. This book will help you acquire the kind of basic information you need to help you be an informed, intelligent participant in your own therapy.

4. *Defeat Depression* can really help you if you *apply* its suggestions. Imagine that you have just read an excellent cookbook. There's a recipe for blueberry pancakes in the book that is particularly appealing. You say to yourself, "I'm going to make those pancakes someday." Now you put the cookbook on a shelf and forget all about it. Subsequently, you meet the author of the cookbook and complain, "You know. I read your book. And I enjoyed it. But I didn't get any blueberry pancakes out of it." Obviously, you must take out a skillet, a box of flour, turn on the stove, obtain some blueberries, and so forth. Otherwise, *no pancakes*. Similarly, you must translate words into action. You must take the coping strategies in the book and, adapting them to your own personality, convert them into realities.

A book and its ideas are Factor 1. You are Factor 2. The positive interaction of Factor 1 and Factor 2 will bring a successful escape from the dismal dungeon of depression.

Key Points to Remember

- It has been said that depression is the common cold of mental and emotional problems.
- Important signs and symptoms of depression include: (1) a general lack of pleasure in life;

(2) distortions in eating behavior; (3) sleep disturbances; (4) disturbances in one's normal activity level; (5) a general lack of energy; (6) the conviction that one leads a useless, ineffectual life; (7) a reduced capacity to think clearly and to solve problems effectively; (8) indirect self-destructive behavior; and (9) preoccupation with thoughts of suicide.

- Approximately seven million adults in the United States are presently struggling with depression.

- The principal kinds of depression are: (1) major depressive disorder, (2) dysthymic disorder, (3) bipolar disorder, and (4) cyclothymic disorder.

- The aim of this book is to help you do precisely what its title indicates: *Defeat Depression.*

2 THE PSYCHOBIOLOGY OF DEPRESSION: BOOSTING THOSE CHEMICAL MESSENGERS IN YOUR BRAIN

Depression is an ancient emotional plague. It has been known and recognized by humankind for centuries.

The Anatomy of Melancholy, published in 1621, is considered to be one of the classic works of literature. Its author was Robert Burton, a librarian and the vicar of St. Thomas, Oxford. The book is a scholarly work bringing to bear a combined knowledge of medicine, literature, and science on the study of depression.

It is, however, possible to reach much farther back in time than the seventeenth century to discover the historical roots of our modern concept of depression. The Greek physician Hippocrates, often called "the father of medicine," identified the features of a depressive syndrome approximately 2,400 years ago. He said that some people suffer from *melancholia*, a tendency to be sad and to feel pessimistic about life.

Biological Factors

The teachings of Hippocrates provide a good starting point for the exploration of biological factors in depression. The great physician asserted that a tendency to have a sour outlook on life is caused by too much black bile. (The Greek root *melanos* means "black"; the Greek root *chole* means "bile.") In general, mood was said to be affected by the balance of "humors" in the body. The word *humor* simply means "fluid." In addition to black bile, the other three humors were *blood*, *phlegm*, and *yellow bile*. Thus, according to Hippocrates, to be in a "good humor" was to have one's body fluids in proper balance.

Although from a modern viewpoint Hippocrates's teachings seem merely quaint and of idle interest, it is worth noting that he was actually on to something. Hippocrates was one of the first thinkers to recognize that mood was tied to natural processes. It was not fate that determined our emotional destiny, but our biology.

This way of looking at things plays a significant role in contemporary clinical psychology and psychiatry. Depression is a problem that is neither strictly biological nor strictly psychological. It is *psychobiological*, meaning that one's mental and emotional life has solid biological underpinnings. Consequently, although the bulk of this book tends to focus primarily on the role that psychological factors play in depression, it is important that we first take a look at the role of biological factors.

What You Can Do

There is much that you can do for yourself at the biological level. One of the good things about this level of intervention is that it is highly accessible. There are very definite actions you can take that will improve the quality of the biological conditions within your body. And this improvement can definitely help you to overcome depression.

TWO CHEMICAL MESSENGERS

Be Aware of Two Key Chemical Messengers Involved in Depression. The biological name for chemical messengers is *neurotransmitters*. Neurotransmitters are complex molecules that are capable, as their name suggests, of sending information from a first neuron to a second one. Neurotransmitters make sensation, perception, thinking, and motor activity possible. (A *neuron* is a cell in the nervous system, including the brain, that specializes in the transmission of information.) The information transmission function of neurotransmitters is the reason they are also called "chemical messengers."

There are two key chemical messengers that have been implicated in depression—*norepinephrine* and *serotonin*. Research suggests that in quite a few cases depressed persons also have low levels of one or both of these two key chemical messengers.

If depression has a primarily biochemical basis due to low levels of norepinephrine and serotonin it is called *endogenous depression*. This term suggests that the depression is due to neither disappointing life circumstances nor psychological factors. Under these circumstances the word *endogenous*, meaning "growing within," is used to suggest the biological roots of some cases of depression.

What causes norepinephrine and serotonin to fall to below-average levels in some people? This is a ticklish question, and does not lend itself to a quick, easy answer. There are various possibilities. Let's take a look at them.

First, it is possible that some people have a genetic makeup that just tends to manufacture low levels of certain neurotransmitters. This of course is the essence of the theory that a tendency toward depression is inherited. Indeed, there is evidence to support this theory. We will return to a consideration of the genetic approach toward the end of this chapter.

Second, it is possible that poor nutrition interferes with the capacity of neurons to synthesize neurotransmitters. Neurons are chemical factories and they make chemical messengers out of organic building blocks. If these blocks are not supplied, it is impossible for the neurons to construct norepinephrine and serotonin.

Third, it is possible that life experiences *do* have an adverse impact on the body's ability to manufacture norepinephrine and serotonin. Although the usual assumption is that low levels of these two substances are due to biological events because they are organic substances, this assumption may, in part, be incorrect. Remember the word *psychobiology*. This suggests that the mind can affect the body and that the body can affect the mind. Consequently, even endogenous depression may be caused to some extent by factors that are not usually identified as biological. We will return to this important point in chapter 4, "Overcoming Learned Helplessness."

The principal function of antidepressant medication, discussed in chapter 9, is to restore either norepinephrine or serotonin to optimal levels. There are, however, other ways to improve the chemical climate in the brain.

B-COMPLEX VITAMINS

Increase Your Intake of Foods Rich in B-Complex Vitamins. As already indicated, neurons need building blocks to manufacture chemical messengers. Evidence suggests that the B-complex vitamins are of particular importance. If your nervous system isn't supplied, via the bloodstream, with an adequate amount of these vitamins, it can't do its job. Consequently, if you take in an ample amount of B-complex vitamins, it is quite possible that you will give your chemical messengers a much-needed boost.

B-complex vitamins consist of a group of related vitamins. That is why they are called a "complex." Eleven vitamins have been identified in the group, including thiamine, riboflavin, niacin, pantothenic acid, and folic acid. It is possible to give a specific list of foods for each individual vitamin. However, in view of the fact that the entire group is important, it is useful to provide one consolidated list.

You will find that these foods are excellent sources of B-complex vitamins:

Avocados

Bananas

Beef, poultry, and fish

Bran

Brewer's yeast

Brown rice

Bulgur wheat

Eggs

Leafy green vegetables

Legumes

Milk

Molasses

Nuts (particularly peanuts, which in fact are a kind of legume)

Soybeans

Wheat germ

Whole grain bread

It is preferable to obtain your B-complex vitamins from natural sources as opposed to tablets or capsules if at all possible. On the other hand, if you are eating highly processed food or grabbing food on the run, you might want to consider taking a daily supplement. Such supplements are widely distributed in drug stores, supermarkets, and health food stores. Read the labels on bottles carefully and make sure that you find a formula that appears to be compatible with your needs.

The taking of large amounts of vitamins for mental health is known as *megavitamin therapy*. It is also called *orthomolecular psychiatry*. (Orthomolecular means the "right" organic molecules.) The approach was pioneered by the biochemist Linus Pauling, a Nobel Prize winner, in association with a psychiatrist named David Hawkins. Large doses of vitamins should not be taken without the advice and supervision of a physician. The reason for this is that some vitamins in large quantities can be toxic. It is usually said that B-complex vitamins are water soluble and nontoxic. However, this does not mean that they can be taken indiscriminately in pill form. A certain amount of prudence is required.

THE "SUGAR BLUES"

Restrict Refined Sugar. Excessive sugar intake provides a kind of reverse image of what happens when we take in foods rich in B-complex vitamins. In particular, Richard Passwater, a research biochemist, notes that the metabolic breakdown of sucrose (ordinary table sugar) makes a heavy demand on niacin, one of the B-complex vitamins. Although all of the data are not in, there is the suspicion that the heavy consumption of ordinary sugar may either induce or aggravate a B-complex deficiency. If this is the case, then the brain's neurons will find it difficult to manufacture both norepinephrine and serotonin. And the individual will experience the "sugar blues," a biochemical depression associated with too much sugar consumption.

Perhaps you are thinking, "Well, I guess this isn't my problem. I don't eat much sugar." Before you get too comfortable with this notion, it is well to consider the concept of hidden sugar. *Hidden sugar* is the not-so-obvious sugar we take in when we eat foods such as cake, pie, cookies, doughnuts, ice cream, candy, jam, jelly, syrup, many breakfast cereals, canned fruit, soft drinks, and even catsup. John Yudkin, a professor of nutrition associated with Queen Elizabeth College of London University, estimates that the average citizen in both the United States and the United Kingdom consumes about two pounds of sugar a week.

Another way in which an excessive amount of dietary sugar can aggravate depression is linked to a condition called *hypoglycemia*. Hypoglycemia is "low blood sugar." Again, the reaction tends to be, "How can taking in sucrose cause *low* blood sugar? It should cause *high* blood sugar, shouldn't it?" The answer to both questions is that, in some people, when too much sugar is eaten the glucose levels in the bloodstream tend to rise rapidly and hit a biological limit or kind of "wall." Table sugar is quickly broken down into glucose. If glucose levels are too high, the hypothalamus, a structure that is a part of the brain, sends messages down the spinal cord to the pancreas. These messages say, "Too much sugar in the blood! Release some insulin to bring things back to normal." Unfortunately, in some individuals the pancreas overreacts and releases too much insulin. This causes the blood sugar to *drop* quickly. The name for this phenomenon is the *hypoglycemic rebound*. In a low blood sugar state the individual loses alertness; arousal is lowered. A sluggish, tired feeling sets in. Anything that significantly lowers central nervous system arousal below optimal levels tends to aggravate depression.

From the biological standpoint, how much sugar do you need to eat? The answer, surprisingly, is *none*. You don't need to eat *any* sugar for your health or physical well being. Sucrose just provides empty calories without nutritional value. Indeed, as we have seen, it tends to deplete your body of important vitamins.

From the psychological standpoint, however, there is a difference. Perhaps you are in the habit of eating certain foods with a lot of sugar content. Perhaps you will feel emotionally deprived if you do not have these foods. And this deprivation can, of course, contribute to depression. Nonetheless, the more you can train yourself, little by little, to restrict your sugar intake, the better you will eventually feel from both a physical and a psychological standpoint.

LIGHT MEALS

Eat Light Meals Whenever Possible. In order to appreciate the importance of this suggestion, let's return to the concept of arousal. *Arousal* refers to a physiological process involving such attributes as the ability to concentrate one's attention and the capacity to work effectively. When arousal is normal, pulse and respiration will be within an optimal range. When arousal is too high, pulse and respiration will increase markedly. When arousal is too low, pulse and respiration will fall well below optimal baselines. Anxiety is associated with excessive arousal. Depression, on the other hand, is associated with low arousal. Consequently, if you have a tendency toward depression, events that contribute to low arousal will aggravate a depressive state.

Arousal is under the control of the *autonomic nervous system*, a division of your nervous system that controls heart action, breathing, alertness, and digestive processes. These are, on the whole, involuntary processes. You can't directly will changes in arousal. You can't sit in a chair and say to yourself, "OK. Now I'm getting more and more aroused. Heart, start beating more rapidly." It just won't work. Arousal can be controlled *indirectly*. For example, you can increase your heartbeat easily by running in place for a couple of minutes.

The subdivision of the autonomic nervous system that increases arousal is the *sympathetic division*. When you are challenged, encounter a novel situation, or are threatened, you will become more alert and ready for action.

The subdivision of the autonomic nervous system that decreases arousal is the *parasympathetic division*. When you are disappointed, tired, or bored, you will become less alert and seek inactivity.

A heavy meal will *automatically* trigger the action of the parasympathetic division of the autonomic nervous system. Blood is diverted to the visceral processes to help you digest your food. As blood leaves the brain and the extremities, you will feel sluggish and lethargic. If you are already a little depressed, *you are going in the wrong direction*. You're headed down a psychological street that won't do you any good. The activity of your parasympathetic division will intensify your depression.

Consequently, as already said, eat light meals whenever possible. If you get hungry between meals, avoid high-sugar foods. A low-calorie, high-protein snack will keep you going, satisfy your hunger, and not interfere with an optimal state of arousal.

SEDATIVES

Limit the Use of Drugs Classified as Sedatives. Sedatives are drugs that, like heavy meals, lower central nervous system arousal. These are the principal sedatives that are likely to be either used or abused:

Alcohol

Barbiturates

Narcotics

Antianxiety drugs

If you drink alcohol because you are depressed, as a form of escape from your emotional misery, you will lower arousal. Lowered arousal will make you more depressed. And you will drink because you are depressed. But you are depressed, in part, because you're drinking. It's a vicious circle, one that is going down, down, down like an airplane in an uncontrollable spin.

Barbiturates are sometimes prescribed to help people sleep. However, if the individual suffers from depression, barbiturates can have an adverse effect. Sometimes the troubled person gets hooked on barbiturates to get through the night. And then he or she gets hooked on amphetamines, drugs classified as stimulants, to counteract the effect of the barbiturates in order to get through the day. Again, a vicious circle has been set in motion.

Narcotics include opium and its derivatives. Derivatives include morphine, codeine, and heroin. (Methadone is a synthetic narcotic. Sometimes it is used in a treatment program to help a person make a break from other narcotics.) The addictive potential of these drugs has been so highly publicized that it doesn't need additional emphasis here. The important point is that narcotics lower central nervous system arousal and aggravate depression.

Finally, antianxiety agents, also known as *minor tranquilizers*, are often prescribed to treat anxiety. You will recall that anxiety is associated with a state of high arousal. Consequently, one of the principal physiological functions of antianxiety agents is to lower arousal. From a pharmacological point of view they are often called *sedative-hypnotics*. They can be very useful drugs if the problem *is* chronic anxiety. But if the problem is chronic depression, they are the *wrong* drug. It is quite likely that an antianxiety drug will act much like alcohol and intensify an individual's depressive state.

A particularly explosive connection is excessive alcohol consumption combined with a psychological dependence on tranquilizers. I recall reading the biography of a famous motion picture actor, a leading man, who combined these drugs. He was found dead in bed in his home in Palm Springs. Suicide was suspected because he did in fact suffer from frequent bouts with depression. However, it is just as likely an explanation to say that he died of physiological shock, a calamitous decline in central nervous system arousal, a kind of extreme coma, induced by the negative joint effects of alcohol and tranquilizers. His behavior may have been suicidal, self-destructive in character, but death was not necessarily his immediate aim.

Suggesting that you limit the use of drugs classified as sedatives is not, in the present context, moral advice. If you suffer from depression, it is realistic advice based on the way in which the central nervous system works.

EXERCISE

Engage in an Exercise Regimen That Is Compatible With Your Personality. Many people say, "I hate to exercise." What they mean, probably, is, "I hate to engage in an activity that I find boring and meaningless." This is reasonable. Consequently, you need to find a way to get your pulse going a little more rapidly at least three times a week that, as is noted above, fits your personality. Look back into your past, perhaps your adolescence. Maybe you liked to play tennis. Or maybe you enjoyed dancing. Or possibly you enjoyed going for long walks. There are, of course, many other possibilities. I, for example, always enjoyed bicycle riding. I still do. As a consequence, I even enjoy using my stationary bike. A friend likes to use a motorized treadmill.

The standard advice is to engage in an activity that will raise your pulse rate about 50 percent over its resting rate. You should engage in this activity three to four times a week for about twenty minutes. I personally find it very motivating to use a pulse meter. This is a relatively inexpensive device available at bicycle shops and electronic stores. A clip attaches to your earlobe and you get a computerized, moment-to-moment display of your actual pulse rate. (If you are over fifty years of age or suspect you have a heart condition, you should consult with a physician before you embark on any systematic program of exercise.)

Why is exercise so important in your efforts to defeat depression? Two important reasons will be specified. First, exercise increases central nervous system arousal. Your pulse increases and you become alert. You wake up your whole system. This is antagonistic to the decrease in central nervous system arousal associated with depression.

Second, exercise appears to foster the production within your central nervous system of endorphins. *Endorphins* are organic molecules that, like norepinephrine and serotonin, act as chemical messengers. (In terms of its roots, the literal meaning of the word *endorphins* is "morphinelike substances arising from within the body.") Endorphins are sometimes said to be natural opiates. This is not meant in a negative sense. On the contrary, the discovery of the body's ability to manufacture its own natural opiates is seen as a useful discovery and a desirable process. By fostering your own body's capacity to generate endorphins you automatically promote antidepressive biological processes.

SUNLIGHT

Obtain Desirable Amounts of Sunlight. Research suggests that, to some extent, depression is linked to changes in the seasons. For example, people are more likely to be depressed in the fall and winter than they are in the spring and summer. Some clinicians identify *seasonal affective disorder (SAD)* as a kind of depression in its own right. However, most investigators regard seasonal variations in mood as a potentially aggravating factor in any one of the types of depression specified in chapter 1.

Studies also suggest that people who live in northern latitudes are somewhat more likely to suffer from depression than are people who live nearer the equator.

What is the common denominator? Note that either winter or living in northern latitudes results in a deprivation of exposure to sunlight. On the other hand, spring and summer as well as living in equatorial latitudes results in an abundance of exposure to sunlight.

It appears that exposure to ideal levels of natural sunlight stimulates the pineal gland to generate optimal amounts of the hormone melatonin. *Melatonin* is, like norepinephrine and serotonin, a chemical messenger. It, like the endorphins, appears to promote a natural sense of well being.

Sunlight has been specified as the best source of light because it contains all of the wavelengths of the visible spectrum, those ranging from red at one end to violet at the other end. The light emanating from most artificial sources is not complete, and just won't do the good job that sunlight does. (However, it should be noted that there are some physicians administering *light therapy*, a therapy that uses lamps that in fact *do* produce all of the important wavelengths.)

Don't overexpose yourself to sunlight. And protect yourself from sunburns. Excessive ultraviolet exposure, associated with sunlight, has been identified as a principal cause of skin cancer. The recommendation, as indicated above, is to obtain *desirable* amounts of sunlight.

How much is desirable? If you live in a sunny climate the amount you obtain during your daily activities, even, for example, as you walk in and out of buildings, might be enough. If, on the other hand, you live in a northern latitude or it is winter, you might want to get out in the middle of the day, when the sun is overhead, for a walk lasting ten to twenty minutes. Individual differences in need appear to vary considerably. And you have to find out by a process of self-discovery what is best for you.

GENETIC FATALISM

Reject Genetic Fatalism. *Genetic fatalism* is the point of view that genes and gene clusters on the twenty-three pairs of chromosomes in every cell of our bodies absolutely determine both our bodily characteristics and our behavioral tendencies. In other words, this is the idea that the tendency toward depression is inherited. More, it is the notion that an unkind fate has dealt you a poor hand of cards, and you are doomed to lose at the game of life even before you begin.

You need to reject genetic fatalism for two reasons. First, it is not good for your mental health. Studies have shown that persons who believe that they have autonomy, real control over their own lives, tend to have a more optimistic outlook than people who believe that they are the victims of fate. This point will be elaborated in chapter 6.

Second, genetic fatalism is *wrong*. It is simply *not* a correct theory of life. In the case of behavior, genes do have a behavioral influence, but not absolute control. Genes *nudge*, but you *decide*. Even sociobiologists, scientists who are powerful advocates of the role that genes play in human behavior, refer to the actions of genes on the human personality as "whisperings." It is as if the genes are whispering in your ear, "Do this now," or "Don't do this now," or "That's not a good idea," or "That was very disappointing." You can hear the whisper, but you don't have to take it to heart. You don't have to act on it. You don't have to *believe* it.

Say to yourself, "It is not the genetic hand of cards I was dealt that is important, but the way I play it. And *this* is under my control."

The Last Word

It is important for you to realize that no unkind biological fate has picked you to be depressed. There is much that you can do for yourself in terms of interventions at the biological level, as this chapter has shown. And future chapters will show you how you can develop the autonomy to either eliminate depression from your life or reduce it from a life-destroying monster to, at the most, an occasionally irritating nuisance.

You really can defeat depression.

Key Points to Remember

- Hippocrates was one of the first thinkers to recognize that mood is tied to natural biological processes.
- Depression is a problem that is *psychobiological* in nature.
- Be aware of two key chemical messengers involved in depression. These are the neurotransmitters *norepinephrine* and *serotonin*.
- If depression has a primarily biochemical basis it is called *endogenous depression*.
- Increase your intake of foods rich in B-complex vitamins.

- Restrict refined sugar. An excessive intake of sucrose is associated with the "sugar blues."
- Eat light meals when possible.
- Limit the use of drugs classified as sedatives.
- Engage in an exercise regimen that is compatible with your personality.
- Obtain desirable amounts of sunlight.
- Reject genetic fatalism.

3 RUMBLINGS FROM THE UNCONSCIOUS MENTAL WORLD: OF RAGE AND DEPRESSION

Daniel H., a forty-three-year-old insurance broker, moved to the edge of his chair and looked at his therapist intensely. "I know why I'm so depressed much of the time and why I drink so much."

Dr. G., an experienced clinical psychologist, responded, "You feel you have insight. You feel you understand what's going on inside of you."

"Yes."

"Go on."

"My father was a doctor. He was a *real* doctor. He cared about people. He was a natural healer. I admired him enormously. He practiced in a rural area with a lot of farms. He even made house calls for emergencies, sometimes at three in the morning. Sometimes I went with him. He was a sort of god to me. And he *loved* me. Yes, he did, he . . ." Daniel's voice became choked.

Dr. G. nodded his head. "You admired him. He was a kind of hero to you."

Daniel nodded and went on. "I was determined to follow in his footsteps. And he expected me to. So did my mother. But when I went to college I just didn't have what it takes. I got B's and C's in premed courses. I goofed off a lot. Partied a lot. I'm not sure if I got bad grades because I goofed off a lot or I goofed off a lot because I just didn't have much natural ability, recognized it, and avoided studying. I think that's it really. Because I know I started out my first year full of enthusiasm."

"How did your father react to your academic performance?"

"He was disappointed. And he let me know it. He told me that this was a golden opportunity, that he was willing to pay all of my bills. But he didn't turn against me. He was willing to support me in another major if I wanted. And this only made me feel more guilty."

"And what happened?"

"I switched from a premed major to an accounting major and eventually got a business degree. But I let him down. And I let myself down." Daniel paused and reflected. "You know, I read the autobiography of Errol Flynn a few years ago. You know, the big movie star popular in the thirties and forties who made a famous version of *Robin Hood*.

"He was a kind of a wild guy in many ways. I'm not like that. I'm a settled family man. I can't identify with that part of his life. But in some ways I'm a lot like he was. His father was an eminent biologist. And he thought Flynn was wasting his life acting in movies. It depressed Flynn to have his father so disappointed in him. And it had a lot to do with his drinking."

"So you feel that if you could have lived up to your father's expectations—"

Daniel interrupted. "My *own* expectations."

Dr. G. said, "Yes, your own expectations, and his as well. If you could have lived up to these expectations, you wouldn't suffer from frequent bouts with depression today."

"That's right."

Daniel's case illustrates one of the ways in which depression can have a psychodynamic basis. A *psychodynamic* explanation of depression is based on the assumption that the self is a battlefield, that a civil war often inflames the personality. This way of looking at behavior is, to a large extent, the result of the teachings of Sigmund Freud, the father of psychoanalysis.

We will return to Daniel's case and the specific kind of problem associated with his depression in a subsequent section of this chapter.

Unconscious Mental Life

Freud asserted that much, perhaps most, of our mental life is obscure to us. This is because of an ego defense mechanism called repression. (In Freudian theory the *ego* is the "I" of the personality, the center of the conscious self.) *Repression* takes place when the ego feels threatened in some way. Psychological information that is likely to be shoved down into the unconscious realm includes (1) painful childhood memories, (2) forbidden sexual impulses, and (3) forbidden aggressive impulses. Almost any mental information that has an adverse impact on self-esteem is likely to be either repressed or distorted in some way.

The unconscious level of the personality can be thought of as a kind of psychological Siberia. Dissident ideas are banished there, but they don't die. They live on and do damage by a sort of psychological remote control. They kick up their heels and exert their influence in numerous ways, making us troubled and bewildered. Freud called this phenomenon the *return of the repressed*.

In order to neutralize repressed ideas it is necessary to make meaningful contact with them, to understand why they are seldom allowed into consciousness and how they can be integrated into a more complete understanding of the self. In order to do this you need to have a more comprehensive understanding of your own unique conflicts and emotional needs.

Coping With Emotional Conflicts

Let's assume that the above description of the operation of the unconscious aspects of mental life is basically correct. If so, we are, in large part mysteries to ourselves. We are masters of self-deception, great at kidding ourselves at our own expense. Consequently, the aim of this chapter is to present a set of strategies that will help you dispel some of the mystery surrounding your own personality. Applying the suggestions presented here will help you get in better contact with what has been called the *hidden self*, the self that lurks just below the level of consciousness. Improved self-knowledge will help to set you free from some of the emotional forces that aggravate depression.

EMOTIONAL CONFLICTS

Accept the Idea That It Is Normal to Have Emotional Conflicts. You don't have to be deeply disturbed and suffer from severe psychopathology to have emotional conflicts. Emotional conflicts are natural for human beings. I have them. You have them. We all have them.

Why? Why do we all have conflicts? The answer resides in the built-in complexity of the human personality. First, applying the psychodynamic theory of personality, it is important to realize that you have what Freud called an *id*, a primitive part of your personality that essentially represents your biological drives, including your sexual and aggressive impulses. The id is pleasure oriented.

Second, you have an *ego*, defined earlier. To repeat, the ego is the "I" of the personality, the center of the conscious self. The ego is reality oriented. It helps you make rational decisions.

Third, you have a *superego*, the social self. The ego is the "we" of the personality. It represents your acceptance of your family's and culture's standards of conduct. The two sides of the superego are the *conscience* and the *ego ideal*. The conscience represents your moral values. The ego ideal represents what you think you should do with your life. (More about this will be presented in a subsequent section of this chapter.) The superego is formed primarily by association with one's parents or parent surrogates, the agents of the larger culture.

The division of the personality into an id, ego, and superego is a very useful device for understanding emotional conflict. In essence the id says, "Go! Do it! It will be pleasurable." The superego says, "No! Don't do it! What you want to do is nasty and immoral." And so you are in conflict.

If you have a strong, reality-oriented ego, you will be able to manage the conflict and maintain an emotional balance. On the other hand, if you are emotionally immature, there may be problems.

Here are a few examples of common emotional conflicts:

Lowell O., a twenty-four-year-old married man with one child, has a crush on his nineteen-year-old sister-in-law, Melinda. He has good reason to believe that he could seduce Melinda. His id nags at him to do it. His superego tells him that he would be a creep to betray his wife and take advantage of Melinda.

Roxanne E., a thirty-three-year-old woman who has been married for nine years, is sick of her overcontrolling mother-in-law. Her id pushes her to tell her off and be outright insulting. Her superego says to keep the peace at all costs. Roxanne knows that if she really speaks her mind she may say too much, and her husband might take his mother's side.

Stella G., a twenty-year-old college student majoring in chemistry, is a virgin. Her boyfriend has been pushing her hard to have sexual intercourse. Being biologically normal, her id says, "It's about time. Go ahead." On the other hand, she is a very traditional person. Her religion's teachings, which she accepts, tell her that sex before marriage is wrong. Consequently, her superego says, "It's a sin to do what you are thinking of doing. Don't!"

Darren I., a forty-four-year-old man, is in the stationery business with his father. Although Darren is married and the father of three children, his father tends to treat him like a child. He has endured his father's manipulation and bossiness for more than twenty years. He feels as if he's selling his soul to his father. His id says, "Tell the old man off. Tell him where to stick his stationery store." His superego says, "What's wrong with you? This is your father! You must *respect* your father. Keep your mouth shut."

ACTING OUT

Don't Act Out Your Id Impulses in an Irresponsible Way. The term *acting out* is used to describe what happens when a person translates the fantasy life associated with the id into actual behavior. If, for example, Lowell does indeed seduce his sister-in-law Melinda, he is acting out.

The *temptation* to act out, energized by the id, causes anxiety. While in a state of emotional conflict, one is nervous because one might or might not do the forbidden or imprudent thing. Consequently one is up in the air. Anxiety is *not* depression. However, it is often a prelude to it.

If you *do* act out an id impulse, then *after* you act out you are likely to become depressed. Depression quickly arises because now the superego is free to punish you. It can say, so to speak, any mean thing it wants to say such as, "You're worthless. You don't deserve to live," or, "You've let everybody down, including yourself," or, "You're a disgusting person," or "You are a filthy sinner."

Note that your superego only has power over you if you actually possess a traditional superego, one that is genuinely shocked by behavior that violates moral standards. If your superego cares nothing for traditional values, you have what clinical psychologists and psychiatrists call an *antisocial personality disorder*, a personality disorder characterized by a general absence of both anxiety and guilt. (An older term for this disorder is *psychopath*. Also, in sociology, the term *sociopath* is often used.) Persons with an antisocial personality disorder don't tend to suffer from the kind of chronic depression being discussed in this book.

In other words, if you get depressed, it is because you have a streak of conscience. It is because you are, basically, a decent person and find it hard to live with yourself when you don't live up to your own higher expectations for yourself.

As a consequence, one way to avoid depression is to look before you leap. Ask yourself, "Will I be able to live with myself after I act on this impulse? What about the morning after? What about the *days* after? Will I regret my actions? What is the long-run price I will have to pay for a brief period of self-indulgence?"

BEING REALITY ORIENTED

Be Reality Oriented in Your Decisions and Your Behavior. Do not conclude from the above paragraphs that you have to throw in the towel and blindly obey the orders of your superego. Perhaps your superego is overly restrictive. Living by its dictates is like trying to function in life while wearing a straitjacket. Your superego should be more like a loose-fitting coat than a too-tight garment.

This is where the ego plays a significant role. The ego is the reality-oriented part of the self that can mediate between the impulses of the id and the dictatorship of the superego. A middle ground can be found. Ernest Jones, a psychoanalyst and Freud's principal biographer, said, "The art of living is the art of compromise."

For example, Roxanne needs to learn how to become more assertive with her mother-in-law. She needs to allow some of her genuine feelings to be expressed without becoming openly hostile.

Darren needs to explore practical ways to escape from his father's domination. Perhaps he should get another job or start a business of his own. He can do these things without openly insulting his father.

There are, of course, times to obey the dictates of a traditional superego. Both Lowell and Stella will almost certainly be better off in the long run if they can inhibit their sexual impulses. Otherwise, they are likely to have to live with regrets. And regrets are a major factor in depression.

In short, from the psychological point of view, you want to behave in accordance with your superego if it is in fact the *realistic* thing to do. Make a *prudent* appraisal of what your id is pushing you to do and what your superego is trying to stop you from doing. Evaluate the long-run payoffs.

If your behavior is realistic, not impulsive or moralistic, you will undercut the roots of depression.

SELF-FORGIVENESS

Learn to Forgive Yourself. Depression often results from the excessive self-criticisms of an overly punitive superego. Don't get too down on yourself. Feelings of guilt, sometimes imaginary or overly intensified, make a person feel worthless. Try to get away from a self-blaming approach. Replace self-blame with a constructive, realistic attitude. Give your attention and energy to the future and what you can *do*, not to the past. We've all heard sayings such as, "What is done is done," and "It's all water under the bridge." Take them seriously. The past is dead. Bury it.

You can, of course, attempt to *atone* for the past. You can make whatever amends are possible. This is a good idea. But note that these are things you can do only in the present and the future.

The devastating results of what happens when a person cannot practice self-forgiveness is the theme of the novel *Ironweed* by William Kennedy. *Ironweed* won the National Book Award in 1983, and was made into a 1987 film starring Jack Nicholson and Meryl Streep. Francis Phelan, the central character, inadvertently drops his infant son on the floor, and the child dies of complications from the resulting injury. This happens many years before the main action of the novel, and is revealed in Francis's nightmarish flashbacks. He becomes an alcoholic and a wanderer. His wife is able to forgive him, and wants him to return home. But Francis cannot forgive himself. He dooms himself to a hell-on-earth existence.

If Francis could learn to forgive himself, then he could live again. An important practical message that can be derived from this novel is: Don't be unforgiving of yourself. Be as kind and forgiving to yourself as you would objectively be toward someone else.

A JOURNAL

Keep a Journal of Your Thoughts and Feelings. It will help you enormously in your efforts at self-understanding to keep a journal of your thoughts and feelings. You don't have to make daily entries; write when the mood strikes you or when you feel a specific need. Putting often chaotic ideas into writing automatically imposes a kind of sense and order on them. Words on paper translate the difficult inner, subjective world of shadows and impressions into an outer, objective world that is somewhat amenable to logic. And logic is one of the prime attributes of the ego, the reality-oriented aspect of the personality.

It is useful in keeping a journal to ask yourself questions. Questions have a way of alerting the mind and inducing it to take a problem-solving stance. Here are examples of the kinds of questions people sometimes ask in their journals:

1. Why was I so hurt when Jack said that he didn't like the way I was dressed tonight? (Jack is the writer's husband.)

2. I got a B on my history test. Its got me down in the dumps. Why? My instructor tells me that a B is a good grade, that she was always happy when she got a B. What makes me think that I have to get straight A's in college?

3. Why do I feel as if I'm nothing and that life is pointless because I'm breaking up with Nancy? How can I go on living and *let go* of her?

4. I feel like I could smash Donovan's face in and bust all of his teeth. I sometimes think I *hate* him. What's going on? The guy has been nothing but good to me. He's paid me well and given me promotions. (Donovan is the writer's employer.)

5. I constantly have sexual fantasies about women other than my wife. Why? One part me says that this is natural. Enjoy the fantasy. Another part of me says that I'm a disgusting specimen of humanity. I feel guilty and miserable and depressed most of the time.

6. It seems to me that other people can always do things better than I can. Or they're better looking. Or they're smarter. Common sense tells me that this general impression is wrong. But why do I persist in feeling this way?

7. Why do I seem to think it's important that everybody like me? Why do I feel down in the dumps at the slightest rebuff or rejection?

Questions like these can be explored more than once until clear thinking prevails.

YOUR DREAMS

Examine Your Dreams. You can include content in your journal arising from your dreams. Some people say that they seldom dream at night. What they almost certainly mean is that they don't *remember* their dreams. Data from sleep laboratories indicate that most adults spend about 20 percent of their night in and out of a state known as *rapid-eye-movement (REM) sleep*. If an average person is awakened in the middle of an REM episode, he or she will usually be able to give a report of a dream.

The trick, then, is to *capture* your dreams. Think of them like butterflies that have to be caught in a net. Your "net" can be a pad and pencil you keep on or near your bed. When you get up during the night to use the bathroom, or when you wake up in the morning, you will frequently remember either a dream or a dream fragment. (REM episodes tend to occur just before we awaken.) Jot down as much as you can.

Later, when you are writing in your journal, transcribe whatever you have jotted down. Then try to add to it. You might even embellish it creatively, a technique recommended by Carl Jung, a pioneer psychotherapist. This embellishment is a kind of dream in itself—a daydream, if you like.

Now you need to make some sense of the dream. Freud said that a dream is the "royal road to the unconscious." It contains useful information about your emotional conflicts that may play a major role in depression. One way to interpret dreams, proposed by Freud in his classical work *The Interpretation of Dreams*, is to make a distinction between the manifest content and the latent content of the dream.

The *manifest content* of a dream is what the dream seems to be on the surface. It is the actual images and events in the dream. Often this is in symbolic form. Consequently, the manifest content contains no transparent meaning. It is as if the dream is speaking to you in code. The *latent content* of the dream is what the dream means. It is what you discover when you *decipher* the dream. The reason that the dream is in code is because the ego is, to some extent, defending itself against the information in the dream. The reason for this defensive action is that the dream often represents a forbidden wish. In terms of one's superego, the latent content is perceived as nasty or evil or immoral.

Gilda O., the mother of three children, had the following dream. A woman in rags is led to a gallows. There is a black hood over her head. The woman is crying. While she is standing on the platform, as the noose is being placed around her neck, a small crowd is yelling insults at her, calling her foul names. Just before the lever is pulled, Gilda wakes up in a sweat, her heart pounding.

This is the manifest content of the dream. Writing about the dream in her journal, and making associations to it, Gilda recognized that the dream was a dream of guilt. She saw that the woman in rags was herself. Why rags? The rags symbolized a degraded status. What was the forbidden wish? It was a strong self-destructive tendency, a tendency forbidden by her superego.

The guilt and the forbidden self-destructiveness experienced by Gilda was linked to the fact that one of her children, Adrian, had almost died of appendicitis when he was seven years old. He had cried and suffered during a long night. Gilda took him to an emergency room in the morning, but she had almost waited too long. The child had peritonitis and eventually recovered after a protracted illness. Gilda nursed her son with great care and he made a full recovery. All of this had taken place three years ago. And she usually tried to avoid consciously thinking about the episode. But her guilt came back to haunt her in her dreams. Interpreting the dream told her that she had not yet completely forgiven herself for her negligence. More important, she needed to come to grips with self-destructive tendencies that interfered with both the quality of her life and her general effectiveness as a mother.

One way to decode the symbols in a dream is to ask and answer questions about them. For example, Gilda wrote in her journal:

1. Why is the woman in rags? This must mean that she's worthless, degraded in some way.

2. Who's face is under the hood? If I take it away, what do I see? Ah, I see *my own face*. The woman on the gallows is me.

3. Why is she on a gallows? She deserves to die. She needs to be punished for the wrong that she has done.

RUMBLINGS FROM THE UNCONSCIOUS MENTAL WORLD

Take Rumblings from the Unconscious Mental World Seriously, But Not Too Seriously. Often when a person first makes contact with repressed ideas and forbidden wishes there is a horrified feeling. "My God, I see that I want to die!" Or, "Good Lord, this means that I hate my wife!" The unconscious domain is like a volcano. It is always rumbling even if it doesn't erupt. The content of the unconscious mental world is like the volcano's heat, fueled by confusion and conflict. It is not correct to conclude, "*I* want to die," or, "*I* hate my wife." This implies that your whole personality is involved. Instead, it is only a *part* of your personality, the id, that wants these "bad" things to happen. Consequently, it is more correct to say, "My id wants me to die" or, "My id hates my wife." The difference may seem small, but in fact it is profound. If you recognize that the id is a kind of blind force, a source of impulses that arise from within you *outside of the action of your will*, it should help you to feel less guilty about some of your feelings.

Freud recognized that the unconscious domain is a kind of Alice-in-Wonderland world where nothing really makes much sense. Consequently, in making contact with it through either reflections or dream analysis in your journal, expect it to be a blurred, confusing, chaotic world. Impose your common sense, your rational powers, on it. Put the id and the unconscious domain where they properly belong: within the sphere of influence of your intelligence and constructive will. As Freud once remarked, "Where id was, there ego shall be."

THE EGO IDEAL

Decide That It's OK to Abandon an Ego Ideal. Let's return to Daniel G., the forty-three-year-old insurance broker introduced in the opening of this chapter. He was disappointed in himself because he felt that he had let down both himself and his father by not becoming a doctor.

Frederick "Fritz" Perls, the principal founder of Gestalt therapy, made an important distinction between *ego ideal actualization* and *self-actualization*. The ego ideal arises from life experiences. It is a kind of artificial graft on the personality. A part of the superego, it does not have inborn roots, but is derived from learning and psychological rewards. Daniel G. observed his father, identified with him, admired him, and received recognition from him when he expressed an interest in following in his footsteps. In this way he acquired the "become a physician" ego ideal.

The need for self-actualization *does* have inborn roots. It is a *natural* part of the personality, and arises primarily from one's own unique talents and potentialities. It represents you yourself and your genuine calling in life. People are self-actualizing whenever they are in the process of becoming the person they were really meant to be. Daniel H. was a natural salesman with an extroverted personality. He had neither the talent nor the aptitude required to become a physician like his father. By becoming an insurance broker he was much more self-actualizing than he would have been by attempting to become a physician.

A conflict between ego ideal actualization and self-actualization can be very distressing. Like Daniel, you are very likely to feel guilty about abandoning an ego ideal that has been nurtured since childhood. However, recognize that you have no real responsibility to become something that is not really a good fit for your interests and talents. Give yourself permission to abandon an ego ideal and it will ease feelings of guilt. This in turn will allow depression to lift.

FRUSTRATION AND AGGRESSION

Be Aware of the Frustration-Aggression-Depression Syndrome. A well-known principle in psychology is the

frustration-aggression hypothesis. The hypothesis states that frustration leads to aggression. Let's say that there is something you want and you can't have it. The natural response is aggression. For example, three-year-old Clarence has just picked up a candy bar in the supermarket. His parent says, "Put it back, Clarence. It will spoil your dinner."

Clarence says, "I want it."

The parent says, "I said put it back."

"No!"

The parent takes the candy bar out of Clarence's hand and puts it back by force.

Clarence is angry. If he is already a relatively socialized child, he may glare at his parent. A less socialized child might say, "I hate you." A really undersocialized child might even kick his parent in the shin. In any event, the *natural* response to frustration is aggression.

We don't really outgrow these tendencies. We just learn to modify them. In life, if we don't get our "candy," we will feel frustrated and angry.

We also feel frustrated when we can't escape from a distressing situation. A child forced to sit still during a visit to a relative's home will be frustrated and feel angry. Likewise, if you feel trapped in a dead-end job or in a loveless marriage, you will have the same kind of feelings experienced by the child.

As already noted, the natural outlet for aggressive impulses is *outward*, away from the self and into the world. However, if you are a decent person, a person with a conventional superego, you will contain many of your aggressive impulses. When aggressive impulses are confined, when they are not expressed, they tend to be a principal causal factor in depression. This is particularly true if the aggressive impulses are repressed to the unconscious domain, if one feels guilty for even having them.

In a psychodynamic context, it has often been said, "Depression is bottled-up rage." And there is quite a bit of truth to this statement.

It is very important that you be aware of the frustration-aggression-depression syndrome. And it is also very important that you *not* feel guilty for what is a natural psychological-emotional sequence.

DISCHARGING AGGRESSION

Find Harmless Outlets for Aggressive Impulses. In the best of all possible worlds you would not be frustrated at all and you would not have the consequent aggressive impulses. In a little better world you would be able to effectively alter your situation, and reduce your level of frustration. Sometimes this is possible. And it is a good idea.

However, in an imperfect world, it is all too often the case that we must remain, at least for a time, stuck in circumstances that frustrate us. Consequently, we will often experience aggressive impulses, meaning we will feel angry or hostile. Under these circumstances, find harmless outlets for your aggressive impulses.

How?

There are a myriad of ways.

The author Raymond Chandler, a man who was frustrated in many ways, wrote tough-guy mysteries about the private eye Philip Marlowe. Marlowe, an outsider, was able to vent his spleen on manipulative women and gangsters. In this way, authors such as Chandler and others, displaced their aggression in a harmless, symbolic form. When aggression is displaced on a work of art, it is called *sublimation*. And it is one way to reduce emotional tension. You may object that you are not an author. I am not suggesting that you are or that you try to become one. But you can write a story meant only for yourself, projecting yourself into the role of the hero. And the hero can act out aggressive impulses that you refrain from acting out in real life.

As indicated, there are numerous ways to discharge aggression harmlessly. Here are a few:

1. Make a painting or drawing that expresses your hostility.

2. Read a novel in which a hero wins out against all odds and defeats a villain. (Novels by Louis L'Amour, for example, fit the bill.)

3. Set up a punching bag. When you are mad, go hit it.

4. Similarly, set up a punch toy, an inflatable, humanlike, thick-skinned balloon. Knock it around when you're angry.
5. Wring a towel and glare at it.
6. Put your anger into words in your personal journal.
7. Write a complaining letter to someone who is frustrating you. After you write the letter, read it over, and then tear it up.
8. If you are alone and can't be heard, growl and grumble under your breath, giving voice to your grievances.

I know that some of these ways of discharging aggression sound rather silly. But they are based on a solid concept in psychodynamic psychology. This concept is called *regression in service of the ego*. You allow yourself to act somewhat like a child in order to keep a better general grip on reality.

All of the examples I have given are far better ways to discharge aggression than to "lose it" and "pop your cork" and do something you really regret. And they are better than living with the depression associated with blocked aggressive impulses.

The Last Word

You *can* cope with your emotional conflicts. It is a matter of finding ways to make self-understanding function constructively in combination with your practical intelligence. By acquiring greater insight into the self it is possible in turn to act more effectively and realistically.

We all have emotions. But they don't have to rule our lives. Say this to yourself, "I have emotions. But they don't have me."

Key Points to Remember

- A *psychodynamic* explanation of depression is based on the assumption that the self is a battlefield, that a civil war often inflames the personality.
- *Repression* takes place when the ego feels threatened in some way.
- Accept the idea that it is normal to have emotional conflicts.
- Don't act out our your id impulses in an irresponsible way.
- Be reality oriented in your decisions and your behavior.
- Learn to forgive yourself.
- Keep a journal of your thoughts and feelings.
- Examine your dreams.
- Take rumblings from the unconscious mental world seriously, but not too seriously.
- Decide that it's OK to abandon an ego ideal.
- Be aware of the frustration-aggression-depression syndrome.
- Find harmless outlets for aggressive impulses.
- Say this to yourself, "I have emotions. But they don't have me."

4 OVERCOMING LEARNED HELPLESSNESS: A NEW LOOK AT THAT DEFEATED FEELING

Edna H., a thirty-seven-year-old married woman with four children, is talking to her best friend, Grace. Last night she had a big argument with her husband. It started with a disagreement about how to discipline their three-year-old son, Danny. But the controversy spread to other issues in their marriage. Edna's other three children are from her first marriage. Her present husband's name is Jackson.

Her drawn face has a woebegone expression. "It's no use trying to work it out with Jackson. Things are just going from bad to worse. It'll all end in divorce in the long run, just like my first marriage to Hunter."

Grace says, "Oh, it can't be *that* bad. You know you love Jackson. And I'm sure from a lot of things that you've said that he loves you. And I can even see it on his face sometimes. You two can work things out."

Edna laughs bitterly. "That's what I used to say about Hunter. And look at what happened. We got to the point where we practically despised each other. No, history is just repeating itself."

"What'll you do?"

"What can I do? I'll just struggle along for a while, I guess. I don't know. I feel like the fly trapped in the web. The struggle is pointless."

Grace says nothing for the moment. She doesn't know what to say.

Edna looks at her with almost no expression. Her whole body conveys the idea that she is a defeated person.

Edna is experiencing a common phenomenon. It is called *learned helplessness*, and we will return to it later in the chapter. For now, focus on the one word *learned*. Learned helplessness can play an important role in depression.

Learning and Depression

Learned behavior is *acquired behavior*. It is acquired by experience. The seventeenth-century philosopher John Locke said that the mind of the infant is like a blank slate. He asserted that there are no inborn ideas. Experience is like the chalk that writes on the slate. The messages written on the slate of the mind, from an emotional point of view, can be negative or positive. And these messages will have much to do with our general outlook on life.

The assertion being made here is that if you are prone to depression, it is quite possible that learned aspects of your behavior may be playing a major role in your responses to life and its many situations.

In this chapter we will look upon depression as a group of habits. A *habit* is a learned response involving a chain of stimuli and responses. It is *unthinking* in its execution. If we just allow self-defeating habits to have their way, they will perpetuate themselves on and on and on. Consequently, we need to look for ways to break or otherwise modify habitual behavior.

Habit Modification

Below you will find a set of self-directed strategies that make it possible to modify habits. By applying these strategies directly to the problem of depression you can effectively undercut its learned roots.

UNLEARNING

Recognize That What Has Been Learned Can Be Unlearned. Habits are not written on stone. Habits owe their existence to the brain and nervous system, a living field of forces that is subject to change and growth. No matter what your age, no matter what the habit, it can be modified.

Extinction is a well-known phenomenon among those who do learning experiments. It is the elimination of a habit. This is what people usually mean when they speak of "breaking" a habit.

It is, of course, often difficult to extinguish a habit. Habits tend to display something called *spontaneous recovery*. You think they're gone, but they come back. However, they can be reextinguished. And, in the end, true extinction becomes a reality. In the case of extinction, the familiar saying, "If at first you don't succeed, try, try again," has real significance.

If a habit cannot be completely extinguished, it can often be *modified*, meaning it can be reshaped in such a way that it causes little or no problem. Consequently, *behavior modification* plays a significant role in today's psychotherapy.

The point is that *there is hope*. Again, what has been learned can be unlearned. Don't shut the door on your own potential for learning—for change and growth.

CUE AVOIDANCE

Avoid Cues That Trigger a Depressive Mood. It is quite likely that you are somewhat familiar with Ivan Pavlov's famous conditioning experiments with dogs. Pavlov sounded a tone of a particular pitch and frequency (popularly called a "bell") *before* feeding a dog. The dog learned to associate the tone with food. Soon when the tone was sounded alone, the dog salivated. Under these

conditions, the tone is called a *conditioned stimulus* and the act of salivating is called a *conditioned reflex*.

John B. Watson, the father of behaviorism, and his research assistant Rosalie Rayner wondered if emotional reactions could also be conditioned. They presented Little Albert, a preschool-age child, with a white rat. The experiment did not begin until Albert was used to the rat's presence and did not try to avoid it. While looking at the rat, a loud gong was sounded behind Albert's head. He was startled, fearful, and began to cry. The next time he saw the rat no gong was sounded. Nonetheless, he cringed, drew away from the rat, and began to whimper. The rat had become a conditioned stimulus. The cringing and drawing away were conditioned reflexes. Watson and Rayner introduced the concept of *conditioned emotional responses* into the psychological literature. These are *learned* responses. (Note that the Watson-Rayner experiment was performed approximately seventy-five years ago, and would be considered unethical in terms of today's professional standards.)

The point is that a depressive mood can be, under certain circumstances, a conditioned emotional response. In the same way that a bell or a white rat can trigger a conditioned reflex, almost any environmental cue has the potential capacity to induce a learned response. A *cue* is a stimulus that you see, hear, smell, or otherwise sense. If the cue has been paired with a depressing experience in the past, it acquires the power, when contact with it is made, to bring forth a depressive mood in the present. Under these conditions, the cue is a conditioned stimulus, and the depressive mood is a conditioned reflex.

Take note of the fact that conditioned reflexes are *involuntary*. They are outside of the control of the will. You can't choose to *not* experience a conditioned reflex when the cue is present. However, and this is extremely important, you can choose to *avoid* cues that you know will trigger a depressive mood. In this manner you, indirectly, take voluntary control over previously involuntary behavior.

From a practical point of view, make a list of cues that may trigger a depressive mood. Work on the list and add to it as you think of cues that at first did not occur to you. Here is a portion of a list put together over several weeks by Grover T., a forty-three-year-old divorced biologist:

1. A spaghetti and meatball dinner with wine. This was our favorite dinner out when Mariel and I dated. Just seeing or thinking about this kind of dinner fills me with unbearable sadness. At first I get a kind of "up" reaction, but then this is quickly followed by a depressive mood. (Mariel is Grover's ex-wife.)

2. Any movie with a prize-fighting sequence. I got beat up once too often when I was a kid in grammar school. (Grover was a short thin child and the victim of bullying.)

3. The smell of pipe tobacco. My so-called best friend Payne used to smoke a pipe. He took advantage of me and manipulated me and *used* me.

4. Almost any romantic ballad that speaks of "love forever" or "caring always" or something like that. I used to *believe* such songs when I was dating Mariel. Now they just make me hurt whenever I hear one.

5. The novel *1984* by George Orwell. This is a great novel and I've read it three times over several years. But why? It always depresses me. It presents a future world characterized by oppression and *no hope*. The main character, Winston Smith, ends up totally defeated. Have I read it because I want to wallow in my misery, because I identify with Winston and misery loves company? Maybe so.

As you can see from Grover's list, cues that trigger a depressive mood are unique to the individual. Make your own list of cues to be avoided. And then do in fact *avoid* them. You will find that you can take control of your depressive moods, to some extent, by applying this straight-forward and logical strategy.

SEEKING OUT CUES

Seek Out Cues That Trigger a Positive Mood. In the same way that certain cues can trigger a depressive mood, other cues, also acquired by association, have the capacity to trigger a positive mood.

Make a list of cues that are likely to trigger a positive mood. Again, work on the list and add to it as you think of cues that at first did not occur to you. Here is a portion of Grover's list:

1. Steve Martin movies when he plays a fool or a jerk. He just makes me laugh.

2. Songs from the musical *Oklahoma* such as "Oh, What a Beautiful Morning," or the title song, "Oklahoma!"
3. A dinner consisting of a broiled steak, a baked potato, and a salad.
4. Time spent with Gloria. (Gloria is Grover's eleven-year-old daughter.)
5. Chatting about biological research with Forest. (Forest is one of Grover's best friends; he is also a biologist.)

Make your own list of specific cues to be sought out. And then do in fact *seek* them. You will find that will become more and more adept at inducing positive moods.

WHEN DEPRESSIVE BEHAVIOR PAYS OFF

Don't Allow Depressive Behavior to Provide You With a Positive Payoff. B. F. Skinner, one of the leading behaviorists of the twentieth century, introduced a concept known as *operant conditioning*. Operant conditioning is a kind of habit formation characterized by an action that results in a consequence for the organism. If the action brings a positive payoff, this payoff is called *positive reinforcement*. An example is provided by Skinner's early research with rats. A rat is trained to press a lever for pellets of food. Pressing the lever is the functional action, or *operant*, and the food is the *positive reinforcer*.

The organism's actions are said to be *instrumental*, meaning that they have a function.

Unfortunately, a depressive action on the part of a human being often has a function. It can sometimes bring a positive payoff. When this happens the depressive action gets *reinforced*, meaning the connection between the action and its payoff is strengthened. And a depressive habit is acquired.

For example, Hazel N. is genuinely depressed one evening. Normally she washes the dishes and cleans up after dinner. But she doesn't feel up to the task. She tells her husband, "Honey, I'm really depressed tonight. Would you be a good sport and do the dishes?"

Her husband, Abbott, a construction worker, has spent a total of two hours driving to and from work, and is tired. Nonetheless, a loving, caring husband, he agrees to do the dishes in the hopes that it will make Hazel feel better.

A few days later Hazel once again doesn't feel much like washing the dinner dishes. This time she isn't depressed, but just finds the task a general nuisance. She remembers how easy it was to get Abbott to do the dishes just by saying that she was depressed. So she tries it again, and it works.

Little by little she falls into the habit of saying she is depressed whenever she wants to get out of cleaning up after dinner. This tendency generalizes to other responsibilities, and she is able to manipulate Abbott into doing more than his fair share of the household chores by constant references to being depressed.

Hamilton and Kendra C. are also a married couple. Hamilton is a temperamental would-be novelist who works as a part-time bank clerk. He has been using the phrase "I'm depressed" for years as a way of avoiding responsibilities in his marriage.

There is a fine line between *being* depressed and *acting* depressed. People who are honestly prone to depression may find, by chance, that acting depressed has positive payoffs. Consequently, he or she may adopt the social role of Depressed Person. (It is a convention to capitalize social roles.) The social role of Depressed Person is an act, a fake front. It does, however, have its origins in genuine depression.

Here is a description of the vicious loop associated with the social role of Depressed Person. In the beginning actual depression induces the individual to act depressed. If this brings a positive payoff, it may eventually induce the role of Depressed Person. Acting out the role makes the person feel more actual depression. And this induces the person to play the role with more frequency. And so on. Therefore the problem gets worse and worse.

Tell yourself, "I will not *use* depression to obtain a positive payoff. I will not resort to depression as a kind of operant behavior. I won't make it an instrumental action." Make a clear distinction between actual depression and the *role* of Depressed Person. Avoid the role and it will help you to also avoid actual depression.

LEARNED HELPLESSNESS

Be Aware of the Difference Between Learned Helplessness and Actual Helplessness. *Learned helplessness* is a concept that was introduced into the field of psychology by the researcher Martin E. P. Seligman. Research on learned helplessness was first conducted with rats, and the rat experiments are instructive because they show how the phenomenon operates at a basic level. Let's say that we have two groups of rats, Group 1 and Group 2. Group 1 is subjected to *escapable shock*. Placed on a shock grid, they are allowed the opportunity to scurry to a safe side of an experimental box. Group 2 is subjected to *inescapable shock*. Placed on a shock grid, they are confined. Their efforts to escape are useless. This is the *training phase* of the experiment.

The *test phase* of the experiment is now introduced. Rats are good swimmers. Place rats from Group 1, one by one, in a deep tank of water. They will swim and swim until they are exhausted. Their experiences in the shock apparatus have taught them that their efforts are generally functional; so they keep trying. Place rats from Group 2, again one by one, in the same deep tank of water. They will swim for only a few minutes, making feeble efforts. They will drown unless they are rescued. Their experiences in the shock apparatus have taught them that their efforts are useless. So they give up without a struggle.

It is evident that the core process in learned helplessness is an overgeneralization. Rats who are actually helpless in a first situation overgeneralize and act as if they are helpless in a second situation, a situation in which they may not be helpless at all.

Seligman and others have demonstrated that the phenomenon of learned helplessness is by no means confined to rats. Research suggests that learned helplessness plays a large and very significant role in human depression.

Lets return to Edna H., introduced at the beginning of this chapter. Edna believed that her second marriage was beginning to turn sour like her first one. She felt helpless and depressed. Edna is a victim of learned helplessness. She suffered a certain amount of actual helplessness in her first marriage because her husband Hunter had an authoritarian personality. He was demanding, overcontrolling, self-absorbed, and inconsiderate. Her best efforts to negotiate differences and to defuse hostility had no beneficial effect on the course of the marriage. She left the marriage discouraged and demoralized.

Edna is now married to Jackson, and she is failing to see that Jackson is a very different man than Hunter. She is overgeneralizing when she tells her best friend, Grace, that history is repeating itself.

Edna is thinking such thoughts as, "All men are alike." What Edna fails to see is that Hunter and Jackson are two *very different* men. They shouldn't be put in the same category. Although Jackson is argumentative at times and has firm viewpoints, he is a person with a generally democratic attitude. He wants to work things out. And he doesn't want to be the boss at all costs. The fact is that Edna is *not* by any means helpless in her relationship with Jackson. And, as Grace, pointed out, he really does love Edna.

Edna needs to say to herself, "I was really helpless in my first marriage. But I'm not helpless now. There's a lot I can do to make this marriage work." She also needs to say to herself, "Jackson is not Hunter. They are two different individuals."

By discriminating actual helplessness from learned helplessness Edna can both overcome depression and save her marriage.

Whenever you encounter a situation in which you feel helpless ask yourself, "Is this actual helplessness or learned helplessness?" Compare *this* situation with earlier situations. It is possible that you will perceive that you are not actually helpless at all now, that you just *feel* helpless because of a natural tendency to overgeneralize. Always attempt to make a distinction between any two situations. Say to yourself, "Situation 1 and Situation 2 are *not* identical. I was helpless once, but I'm not helpless now."

LEARNED OPTIMISM

Recognize That Learned Optimism Is Naturally Antagonistic to Learned Helplessness. Seligman's continuing research demonstrated that in the same way people acquire learned helplessness, they can acquire *learned optimism*. Learned optimism takes place when a successful experience in a first situation is generalized to a second situation. For example, Flint V. is a psychology major. It is his junior year in college. He takes his first course in statistics with fear and trembling because, as he says to himself, "I was never good at math." (Note that he is suffering from a certain amount of learned helplessness arising from some negative experiences in math classes in high school.)

Flint is gratified to find out that in fact he can do the required work in statistics fairly readily. The adult he is now is not the adolescent he was in high school. His study skills are better and he is motivated. He earns a semester grade of B in the statistics class. Consequently, he approaches his second statistics class with a positive mental attitude. He believes in his ability to master statistical concepts if he just applies himself. Now Flint is experiencing learned optimism. And, if success begets success, as it often does, Flint will become more and more self-confident about his statistical competence.

REINFORCE LEARNED OPTIMISM

Discover Ways to Reinforce Learned Optimism. Optimistic behavior is a kind of operant behavior, meaning behavior that is purposive. And the purpose is to obtain a positive reinforcer, a psychological reward. If you want learned optimism to become a stronger and stronger force in your life, counteracting learned helplessness, be sure to load the behavioral dice in your favor. In other words, set yourself up for successful experiences, not failure experiences.

When an action leads to a successful consequence, then that action is automatically reinforced. The B that Flint received in his statistics class was a positive reinforcer. Even a small success can be highly reinforcing. Think of small successes as stepping stones on the pathway toward larger successes. In Flint's case, the B in statistics points in the direction of a degree in psychology.

Here are a few pointers that will help you reinforce learned optimism:

1. *Don't bite off more than you can chew.* Often, in an attempt to counteract learned helplessness, people go overboard. Penelope G., a single parent, returned to college as an adult, took a full load of 15 semester units, worked as a waitress 25 hours a week, and mothered three children. She dropped out of all but two classes, and earned a C and a D in those classes. She succeeded in reinforcing not learned optimism, but learned helplessness. She "proved" to herself that her dream of becoming a college graduate was an impossibility.
2. *Be patient.* Remember the old saying, "Rome wasn't built in a day." How was it built? Stone by stone. So learn to pace yourself and don't get too

excited. If for example, you start a business, don't expect it to be a big success overnight. Nurture it the way you would a small plant. It takes time for anything to thrive. Expect good results if you put forth the right kind of effort, but don't expect near-instant results.

3. *Actively reject Murphy's Law*. Murphy's Law is often quoted by persons who suffer from learned helplessness. They say, "If anything can go wrong, it will." Consciously say to yourself, "Murphy's Law is *wrong*." Let's invent a new law and call it the *Anti-Murphy Law*. The Anti-Murphy Law says, "If anything can go right, it might. Why not?" Memorize this new law and mentally recite it when you are tempted to thoughtlessly repeat the original Murphy's Law. Use the Anti-Murphy Law like a kind of psychological anti-matter, a force that knocks out the old law.

4. *Dream possible dreams, not impossible ones*. One of the characteristics of persons who suffer from learned helplessness is that they set a level of aspiration either too low or two high. They settle for little or nothing or they "shoot for the moon." In *Man of La Mancha* Don Quixote sings of "dreaming the impossible dream." Although this is quite romantic and appealing, it makes no real sense. In order to reinforce learned optimism you must focus on dreaming *possible* dreams. So have goals, yes. But place them within reach. They shouldn't be too easy to reach. If so, reaching them will not be gratifying. Nor should they be so difficult to reach that they are in fact *out of reach*.

Apply these four principles to the acquisition of learned optimism, and you will be gratified with the results. You *can* convert learned helplessness into learned optimism.

LEARNED HELPLESSNESS AND CHEMICAL MESSENGERS

Be Aware That Learned Helplessness Is Likely to Affect the Levels of Key Chemical Messengers. In chapter 2 it was pointed out that low levels in the brain and nervous system of the chemical messengers norepinephrine and serotonin were associated with depression. Usually it is assumed that these low levels are a cause of depression. But what causes the low levels? It is commonplace to assign this to biological factors such as genes or nutrition. These possibilities were discussed in chapter 2.

Recent research with animals has suggested that when their training experiences induce learned helplessness, their brains and nervous systems don't generate normal levels of the two key neurotransmitters. (Keep in mind that learned helplessness is a major factor in depression.) These results suggest, broadly speaking, that it is just as true to say that depression causes low levels of important chemical messengers as it is to say, according to convention, that low levels of important chemical messengers cause depression.

We seem to have a chicken-and-the egg problem. What causes what? In reality there is no problem. Causation can be a two-way street. Factor A can have a causal influence on factor B. And factor B can in turn have a causal influence on factor A. Technically, this is called an *interaction*, meaning that the joint effects of two variables can be complex. Chemical messengers and learned helplessness interact. Consequently, one of the practical ways to boost the key chemical messengers in your brain is to extinguish the habit of learned helplessness and replace it with the habit of learned optimism.

ACTION AND FEELING

Act Less Depressed and You Will Feel Less Depressed. Common sense tells us that feelings act as motives.

Logically then, it would seem that feelings come first, followed by actions. You see a bear in the forest and run away. Fear motivates the running. You feel depressed and you engage in depressive behavior (you listlessly hang around the house all day in an old bathrobe).

Nonetheless, common sense can be turned on its head. A basic tenet of behavioral psychology is that feelings flow from actions as much as actions flow from feelings. For example, in assertiveness training, people are encouraged to *act* more assertively even when they don't *feel* assertive. Interestingly, little by little, persons who will themselves to act assertively begin to feel more self-confident. They "become" their actions.

Similar logic applies to depression. You can't directly control your feelings by an act of will. You can't say to yourself, "Be less depressed today." But you *can* control your actions by an act of will. You can say to yourself, "I'm going to take a shower, get out of this bathrobe, and leave the house." If you make yourself act *as if* you are not depressed, then, sometimes, depression tends to lift.

Note that I have included the word *sometimes* in the above sentence. I don't want to oversimplify and give the impression that acting less depressed is a cure-all for depression. Nonetheless, it can be an important weapon in your fight against low moods. And you should take advantage of the general principle whenever possible

The Last Word

The learned aspects of depression are of great importance. To a large extent, depression can be looked upon as a pathological habit. Conditioned emotional reactions and learned helplessness play significant roles in this habit.

This chapter has provided you with practical ways to either extinguish (break) or modify useless habits associated with depression.

Again, remember that what has been learned can be unlearned. You really can replace learned helplessness with learned optimism and consequently, to repeat a key word, *learn* to defeat depression.

Key Points to Remember

- In this chapter depression was looked upon as a group of self-defeating habits.
- Recognize that what has been learned can be unlearned.
- If a habit cannot be completely extinguished (broken), it can often be *modified*, meaning it can be reshaped in such a way that it causes little or no problem.
- Avoid cues that trigger a depressive mood.
- Seek out cues that trigger a positive mood.
- Don't allow depressive behavior to provide you with a positive payoff.
- Be aware of the difference between learned helplessness and actual helplessness.
- Recognize that learned optimism is naturally antagonistic to learned helplessness.
- Discover ways to reinforce learned optimism.
- Be aware that learned helplessness is likely to have an adverse effect on the levels of key chemical messengers.
- Act less depressed and you will feel less depressed.

5 DEPRESSING THOUGHTS: USING REASON AGAINST MELANCHOLY

Here are the opening paragraphs of *The Man Who Thought Too Much*, an unpublished autobiographical novel by Paxton L., one of my counseling clients:

> *When Quentin Radcliff got out of bed that morning his first thought was, "Why am I getting out of bed? I know it's going to be a lousy day." While he was shaving, he thought, "I look awful this morning. My eyes are puffy and swollen." Driving to work he thought, "I'm facing a ton of work today. I doubt if I can even get half of it done." And he continued on that way for the rest of the day.*
>
> *Every thought was negative. And he was a very depressed, unhappy man.*
>
> *The days followed the days in a gray, sad sameness.*
>
> *And then one day a young woman named Malva was hired to be his assistant. Her bright, shining eyes and ready smile disturbed him. She insisted on looking at everything in an upbeat way. And Quentin thought, "She's trouble, nothing but trouble."*

As you can see from the excerpt, Quentin depressed himself with his own thoughts. Quentin, of course, is a projection by Paxton of himself into a fictional form.

Many people who suffer from depression have much in common with the protagonist of *The Man Who Thought Too Much*. They make themselves emotionally ill and destroy the quality of their own lives by constantly repeating ideas to themselves that are dismal and self-defeating.

Cognitive Therapy

An important trend in contemporary psychotherapy is an emphasis on the importance of examining and reevaluating one's own thoughts. This trend goes by several names. Albert Ellis, a New York psychotherapist, originally called his own system *rational-emotive therapy*. (He now calls it *rational-emotive behavior therapy*.) Behavioral psychologists speak of *cognitive-behavior modification*, meaning that cognitions, or thoughts, are learned behaviors, like other behaviors, and are subject to behavior modification. Aaron T. Beck, a professor of psychiatry, uses the term *cognitive therapy*. All three terms mean approximately the same thing. For convenience, I will use the term cognitive therapy.

Let's define cognitive therapy as follows: An approach to therapy that teaches a client to take voluntary control of his or her own thoughts in order to gain indirect control of mood states such as anxiety, anger, and depression.

Coping With Your Own Thoughts

The good thing about cognitive therapy is that it lends itself readily to practical self-applications, strategies that you can begin to use right away to help you defeat depression.

AUTOMATIC THOUGHTS

Learn to Identify Automatic Thoughts. According to Beck, *automatic thoughts* are ideas that appear in consciousness more or less unbidden. They tend to be rapid, often flashing in and out of the mental spotlight very quickly. If they contain a negative outlook on life, as they often do, then they act as a kind of psychological poison. This poison spreads throughout the personality inducing a state of depression.

Because automatic thoughts play such an important role in human depression it will serve you well to be able to identify your own automatic thoughts. You will be better able to do this by becoming familiar with certain key characteristics of automatic thoughts.

First, they are *well defined*. In view of the fact that they occur in the form of sentences that you consciously run through your mind, they actually say something. Examples already given from *The Man Who Thought Too Much* provide evidence of the shape of automatic thoughts.

Second, they are *autonomous*, meaning they have a kind of life of their own. They arise, as already indicated, unbidden. It would seem that they come from the subconscious level of human experience, leap into conscious mental life briefly, and drop down into the subconscious pool again. There they prime themselves for future darting, and disturbing, entries into our conscious worlds.

Third, automatic thoughts are *superficially plausible*. On the surface, they will seem rational to you. You will think of them as correct appraisals of life and its varied situations. As you will see, this view of automatic thoughts is both incorrect and harmful.

Fourth, automatic thoughts are *personal*. They are *your* thoughts, not someone else's. Consequently, they tend to focus on those situations and people who are of paramount interest in your life.

Although automatic thoughts are called "thoughts," one might go so far as to say that they are not, in a sense, thinking at all. They are *mental conditioned reflexes*. A stimulus triggers one of them, and the thought runs itself off in a predictable chain reaction. Consequently, you will have the same automatic thought over and over again as the days follow the days. If the thought is a negative one, it will contribute to persistent depression.

CAPTURING AUTOMATIC THOUGHTS

Capture Your Automatic Thoughts. Automatic thoughts are like flying fish. They leap out of the mind's subconscious pool into the "air" of consciousness. They flash by. And then they plop down into the pool again and sink temporarily out of sight. You may quickly forget that you had the thought at all. Nonetheless, the damage has been done. And your mood has been affected.

Consequently, it is a good idea to capture automatic thoughts as they flash by. You need a "net." The most practical net is a piece of paper and a pen or pencil. When the thought zips through your conscious mind, observe it, recite it to yourself in order to fix it, and then write it down at the first opportunity. Here is a short list of negative automatic thoughts that I have acquired from various counseling clients:

"My children neglect me." (The writer has three daughters and a son, all married adults.)

"Life is the pits."

"I am never going to amount to anything."

"I really made a fool out myself last night."

"Death makes life meaningless."

"It's not what you know, it's who you know."

"You can't win no matter how hard you try."

"I am taken for granted all of the time by everybody."

"I'm a total failure."

CHALLENGING THOUGHTS

Challenge Automatic Thoughts. Once automatic thoughts have been captured they can be scrutinized and evaluated in the cold light of logic. Shine a harsh beam of rational analysis on them and they tend to wither and shrink, losing much of their power to influence you and induce depression.

In order to challenge automatic thoughts, it will be helpful to you to be familiar with Ellis's ABC system of emotional self-control. Ellis says that mood states tend to proceed along the lines of the following pattern. First there is A; this stands for the *activating event*. This is something that you see, hear, or otherwise actually sense. It is *outside* of the self. Second there is B; this stands for the *belief* about the event. A belief is *within* the self. Beliefs that cause emotional trouble are called *irrational beliefs* by Ellis. (They are the same as automatic thoughts.) Third there is C; this stands for the *consequence* of the belief. The consequence in this case is an *emotional* consequence. So read point C as "emotional consequence." In this case, of course, the reference is to a depressive mood.

Most people stop at point C. They just don't go past the mood. They are depressed and they feel that the mood state is justified in terms of their belief system. Ellis points out that a belief system is *perceptual*. It is an evaluation of A, the activating event; but it is not the event itself. Therefore, a belief—shaped by an automatic thought—is subject to modification. The mental sentence can be rewritten. And this can alter the mood in a positive direction.

Therefore Ellis recommends that we introduce a point D into the mental process I have been describing. The D stands for *dispute*. Dispute the truth of the irrational idea represented by point B. Or, in other words, *challenge* it. Don't take its correctness for granted.

Disputing or challenging one's own thoughts is not a common characteristic of the average person's mental life. On the contrary, it is simply something that most people *don't* do. But the fact that the behavior is not common doesn't mean that it can't be done. It really is possible by an act of will to look at your own thought processes and bring them under better rational control.

COGNITIVE DISTORTIONS

Become Familiar With the Principal Cognitive Distortions. You will be much more able to successfully challenge the content of your automatic thoughts if you become familiar with the principal cognitive distortions.

Cognitive distortions are ways in which your thinking becomes warped; and this warping in turn has an adverse impact on your mood states. Below are listed the principal cognitive distortions.

Either-or thinking. This kind of thinking is characterized by acting as if everything that is experienced falls into one of two categories such as "good" or "bad," "right" or "wrong," "success" or "failure." In the list of automatic thoughts provided earlier, the statement, "I'm a total failure" gives an example of either-or thinking. The individual is seldom a *total* failure or success. The writer of the statement had many individual successes and many individual failures. She was successful as a mother, but a failure as a businesswoman. Although this failure *is* a disappointment, she is boxing life too rigidly by employing either-or thinking.

Overgeneralization. To overgeneralize is to select a single instance and make it the basis for a sort of "law" or rule. It has also been called *false allness*. You are taken advantage of by a person with curly hair. You meet a second person with curly hair and think, "You can't trust people with curly hair." In the list presented earlier, the automatic thought "My children neglect me" provides an example of overgeneralization. You will recall the writer had three daughters and a son. The fact was that, like most adult children, they were sometimes thoughtful and sometimes neglectful.

Disqualifying the positive. If you disqualify the positive, you tend to shortchange the positive features of an experience. In the list presented earlier, the statement "Death makes life meaningless" provides an example of disqualifying the positive. The individual with the thought was neglecting to assign any value to the simple everyday joys of life such as watching a child take his or her first steps, listening to a bird's song, or enjoying a good meal.

Another example is provided by the general approach to life of Bryce R., a thirty-two-year-old software engineer who has never been married. He can always find the flaw in anything. He sees a movie and thinks, "The plot had too many coincidences." He eats a meal in a restaurant and thinks, "The steak was cold." He buys a pair of slacks and later is disappointed, thinking as he looks in a home mirror, "The pleats are too full." This, of course, is in part the reason he has never married. He can readily see something wrong in every woman he meets.

Magnification of other people's successes. When you magnify other people's successes, you also tend to minimize your own. You get a promotion and think, "It's nothing." Somebody else gets a promotion and you say, "She's on her way!" You get an A on an examination and think, "So what. It's a fluke." Somebody else gets an A on a test and you think, "He really has a lot of ability." You tend to see yourself as inferior and others as superior. This, of course, is not reality. It's your thinking *about* reality that is distorting your perception.

Should-have statements. Should-have statements usually begin, "I should have . . ." Obviously, they are a way of punishing yourself. You think, "I should have bargained for the car. I paid too much." Or, "I should have worn a better dress to the party last night. I looked stupid the way I was dressed." Or, "I should have been a better parent." Or, "I should have studied harder when I had the chance to go to school." As you can see, should-have statements tend to be past oriented. They are, consequently, *useless* and *futile*. They are a form of mental masochism that can only make you feel worse and worse.

Personal labeling. Personal labeling occurs when you attach a label to yourself. It is a form of name calling, and you are doing the name calling. You think, depending on events and circumstances, "I'm a jerk." Or, "I'm as fat as a house." Or, "I'm a loser." Or, "I'm a blockhead." Personal labeling, like making a should-have statement, is a way of dumping on yourself. It is an inner judge that scrutinizes you too closely and too harshly.

In *transactional analysis*, a personality theory, this inner judge is called the Parent ego state. (It is a convention to capitalize the word *parent* in order to distinguish the ego state from an actual parent.) The Parent ego state is likely to be somewhat severe if your actual parents were authoritarian and overcontrolling. This is frequently a feature to be found in the case histories of persons who suffer from depression. (There will be more about transactional analysis in chapter 7.)

Personalization. Personalization takes place when you take another person's worries on your shoulders. You are trying to help someone else through a rocky marriage, a major financial readjustment, a problem in raising a child, or studying for an important examination. If the individual succeeds, you are modest and take little or no credit. However, if the person fails, you place all of the responsibility on yourself. You think, "I should have tried harder." Or, "I let Mary down." Or, "I guess I wasn't any help."

As you can readily see, automatic thoughts warped by cognitive distortions contribute greatly to depression. Therefore, you want to scrutinize your own thought processes and work at ridding yourself of cognitive distortions.

INTERRUPTION

Employ Thought Interruption as a Cognitive Skill. A skill associated with cognitive therapy is called *thought interruption*. Although negative automatic thoughts tend to follow one another in a kind of mental domino effect, your mind doesn't have to work that way. You have options. Research with cognitive therapy has shown that it is possible for subjects to voluntarily take control of their thoughts and interrupt a sequence of ideas.

One way to do this is to run a movie in your mind's eye. When you catch yourself thinking a series of automatic thoughts, visualize a hand holding the handle of a large white and red sign that says: "STOP!" See the hand and sign pop up, as if from a jack-in-the-box. And then think, "I want to obey this sign. I'm going to stop this self-defeating series of automatic thoughts. They have no function other than to make me depressed."

SUBSTITUTION

Employ Thought Substitution as a Cognitive Skill. Another skill associated with cognitive therapy is called *thought substitution*. You can use this skill immediately after using thought interruption. When a mental sequence has been interrupted, in order to keep yourself from returning to it, voluntarily introduce a new thought, a thought that is antagonistic to the negative automatic thought. Every negative thought has its positive opposite. Make an effort to find the positive opposite and then *think it*.

Referring to the list of automatic thoughts presented earlier, here are a few examples of reversal thoughts that can be used in the substitution process:

Automatic thought: "I am never going to amount to anything." *Logical opposite*: "I'm going to be somebody someday."

Automatic thought: "I really made a fool out myself last night." *Logical opposite*: "I had a lot of fun with my friends last night."

Automatic thought: "Death makes life meaningless." *Logical opposite*: "Life has intrinsic meaning and purpose."

Automatic thought: "I'm a total failure." *Logical opposite*: "I'm often successful at the things I do."

Perhaps you object, "But the logical opposites are not true. How can you think them if they're not true?" There are three responses to these objections. First, the automatic thoughts aren't true. They aren't congruent with reality. They represent, as already indicated, irrational ideas and cognitive distortions. Second, logical opposites to automatic thoughts are just as "true" as the automatic thoughts. In the mental domain "truth" is a fuzzy word. To some extent, thinking makes truth and reality. If you act as if something is true, it often becomes so. Actions can convert ideas into self-fulfilling prophecies. Third, you can think anything you want to think. Thinking is private and entirely under your control. You don't *have to* think those thoughts which destroy your joy and aggravate your depression.

The Last Word

Cognitive therapy and the personal interventions presented in this chapter have a solid basis. That basis is an ancient philosophy known as *stoicism*. Stoicism is the point of view that it is not circumstances themselves, but our thoughts about them, that make us happy or sad. These thoughts affect our perceptions and our emotional states. The stoic philosophers recognized that we could not take direct control of either our perceptions or our emotions. But they asserted that we *can* take direct control of our thoughts.

Epictetus, a principal founder of stoicism, said almost two thousand years ago, "First, say to yourself what you would be; and then do what you have to do." Applying Epictetus's dictum to this chapter, you first say to yourself that you want to defeat depression; and then you voluntarily think the thoughts that will accomplish this goal.

Key Points to Remember

- *Cognitive therapy* teaches a client to take voluntary control of his or her own thoughts in order to gain indirect control of mood states such as anxiety, anger, and depression.
- The good thing about cognitive therapy is that it lends itself readily to practical self-applications, strategies that you can begin to use right away to help you defeat depression.

- Learn to identify automatic thoughts. *Automatic thoughts* are ideas that appear in consciousness more or less unbidden.
- Capture your automatic thoughts.
- Challenge automatic thoughts.
- Become familiar with the principal cognitive distortions. *Cognitive distortions* are ways in which your thinking becomes warped.
- Employ thought interruption as a cognitive skill.
- Employ thought substitution as a cognitive skill.

6 ESCAPING FROM A WASTELAND: TOWARD THE DISCOVERY OF MEANING IN LIFE

Do you feel that you are becoming the person you were meant to be?

Do you feel that your life has meaning and purpose?

We'll return to these two questions in the next section of this chapter.

One of the most famous poems of the twentieth century is *The Waste Land* by T. S. Eliot. Published in 1922, it is thought by many readers to capture an essential theme in industrialized society. The barren world described in Eliot's poem refers to the general civilized world of the modern person. However, it is also an *inner world*. It is a spiritual landscape, a psychological world devoid of joy. Eliot's writing describes an existence scorched of pleasure. (Although Eliot uses two words, I will follow the convention of using *wasteland* as a one-word term.)

Eliot's poem is important because it had the effect of increasing the general level of human consciousness concerning an important and growing problem, the problem of the demoralization associated with a loss of meaning in life. However, Eliot's poem is limited because it spells out no pragmatic solution to the problem it describes. It leaves the reader feeling helpless and hopeless.

It is worth pointing out that Eliot himself suffered from depression and was treated for it. From the psychological point of view, Eliot's poem can be thought of as a projection. *Projection* is an ego defense mechanism in which the individual perceives the outer world in terms of an emotional conflict or mood state. It seems evident that Eliot's description of the modern condition as a wasteland tells us as much about Eliot's state of mental and emotional health as it tells us about the actual state of the modern world.

Existential Depression

Returning to the opening questions of the chapter, how did you answer them? If you answered no to either or both questions, it is quite possible that you are suffering from an existential depression. An *existential depression* is present when an individual feels as if life contains nothing of value. Everything seems pointless and without purpose. It is, quite literally, a depression concerning one's very *existence*. (An existential depression is not one of the formal clinical categories specified in Chapter 1. It is, however, generally understood by mental health professionals to play a major aggravating role in clinical depression.)

In one of his songs the lyricist Oscar Hammerstein II asked, "Why was I born? Why am I living?" A person suffering from an existential depression might answer, "I don't know why I was born. I go on living—if you can call dragging along living—because of habit."

On the other hand, a person who is fully functioning might answer, "I was born to enjoy my life and accomplish something. I am living to complete some projects that are very important to me and to raise my children."

An existential depression is not a *must* of modern life. It is a *risk* of modern life. And if you have fallen into the emotional hole of an existential depression, you can climb out.

You are *not* helpless. And the situation is *not* hopeless.

Helping Yourself

Below you will find practical ways to cope with an existential depression. An important precondition to effective coping is the *belief* that you actually do have the potential power to cope. William James, a principal founder of American psychology, fell into an existential depression early in his career. He believed at that time that we are pawns of natural law, that all of our behavior is determined by biological and environmental forces beyond our control. Then he read some essays on free will by the philosopher Renovier; these essays convinced James that free will was a reality. He said that his first act of free will would be to believe in free will. And with this decision his depression began to lift.

So make it a point right now to believe that you have voluntary control over your own behavior. This belief will help you employ the strategies to be recommended.

THE PSYCHOLOGICAL WORLD

Realize That You Live in a Psychological World. The Gestalt psychologist Kurt Koffka made an important distinction between the *geographical world* and the *psychological world*. The geographical world is the world as described by physics. It is the actual, natural world that is really *out there*. The psychological world is the world of perception, the world as represented in your mind. Although it may seem that somehow the geographical world is more "real" in some way, it is the psychological world that determines your behavior. And consequently, in terms of your actions and emotions it is more important.

Koffka gives the following example. A man is traveling on horseback at night in West Germany during a blizzard. He crosses an expanse covered by drifts of snow. He sees a light and arrives at an inn. The innkeeper asks from what direction he has come. The voyager says, "From the north."

The innkeeper says, "My God, man. Do you realize that you have just crossed over a portion of Lake Constance? The ice is very thin this time of year. You have barely escaped with your life!"

Upon receiving this news, the traveler becomes so agitated that he falls into a faint and almost has a heart attack.

Obviously it is the psychological world that determined his behavior, not the geographical one. The psychological world contained solid ground. The geographical one, thin ice. The man acted in terms of what he *believed* about the world, not the world as it actually was.

The point of all this is that the psychological world is your *construction*. There is no objective "is-ness" to it. It "is" what you think it is. If you believe that life is empty and pointless, then it "is." If you believe that life is full and meaningful, then it "is."

By realizing this important point, you are free to construct a psychological world that meets your emotional needs. There is nothing new or radical about this viewpoint. It is spelled out quite completely in the philosopher Arthur Schopenhauer's *The World as Will and Idea*, published more than 150 years ago.

The importance of one's psychological world is also conveyed in Frank Capra's 1946 film *It's a Wonderful Life*. George Bailey, played by James Stewart, thinks that it "is" a terrible life and wishes he had never been born. Then a series of experiences convince him that it "is" a wonderful life, and he's glad he was born. The objective world, the world *out there*, remains the same before and after. All that has shifted is George's point of view, his outlook on life.

The self-directed strategies that follow will help you modify your psychological world in such a way that you perceive it to be open and bright instead of confined and gloomy.

SELF-ACTUALIZATION

Become More Self-Actualizing. The humanistic psychologist Abraham Maslow said that we all have an inborn need for self-actualization. *Self-actualization* is the need to become the person you were meant to be. (This need refers to one of the two questions asked at the opening of this chapter.) Another way to define self-actualization is to say that it is the need to maximize your unique talents and potentialities. Every one of us has a need to grow as a person. If we ignore this need, if we neglect it and don't nurture it, we tend to fall into a depressive mood.

Maslow provides the example of a young woman who dreamed of becoming a psychologist. She was a college graduate and an assembly-line supervisor in a chewing gum factory during the Great Depression of the 1930s.

She was the only person in her family who could find a job, and she was burdened down with responsibility. And she confessed to Maslow that she was depressed.

Maslow says that she was short-circuiting the need for self-actualization in the name of responsibility. He advised her to keep her job for the time being, but to also go back to graduate school and work toward her long-range vocational goals. He said that this was important even if she had the time and energy to take only one class a semester. The important thing was not to let her dream die, to feel that she was at least in some part engaged in making it into a reality. The young woman took Maslow's advice, and her depression lifted.

Many people are not self-actualizing because they think that actions associated with the process are "impractical." It is true that being self-actualizing often won't make you any money. But what could be more impractical than allowing yourself to fall into a depression?

In order to find out what self-actualization means to you on a personal basis you need to look into yourself. You have to ask yourself, "What do I have a natural talent for doing? What did I dream of becoming as a child or as an adolescent? What activities give me great joy? Then free your mind of external distractions and *listen* to the answers it gives to the questions. Maslow spoke of *impulse voices*, natural whisperings within our own consciousness. The mythologist Joseph Campbell uses a somewhat different language. He speaks of "following your bliss." Most of us intuitively understand what Maslow and Campbell are talking about because self-actualization appears to be an *inborn* need.

Here are some statements collected from several counseling clients who decided to become more self-actualizing:

"I loved to paint as a child. Although I am a hard-working accountant, I decided to take an evening oil painting class at a local community college. It was one of the best decisions of my life. I look forward to the time I spend in front of the easel. It does a lot to refresh me and keep me going."

"I have always loved to both act and sing. I appear in local productions. Recently I played one of the three sisters in *Fiddler on the Roof.*"

"I've been wanting to write novels for I don't know how long. I put the whole thing aside for years because I was too busy earning a living and raising children. Then I began writing a novel on the kitchen table. I can only find the time to write one or two pages a day. But this is enough. I can write a novel a year this way, and who can ask for more?"

"I love to create my own recipes. Lately I've been setting aside Saturday mornings for this activity, and I'm really enjoying it. I came up with my own concoction recently, a chocolate cake with marshmallows and almonds, and my friends and family really like it. I'm thinking of entering it in a contest."

"I'm learning to reupholster furniture. I'm getting a bang out of selecting fabrics and giving old things a new lease on life."

"This may sound ridiculous, but I've always wanted to know how to tap dance. I'm taking tap dance lessons, and it's great fun."

You will notice that a creative element enters into most self-actualizing activities. This is because the need for creativity is a natural part of the human mind, and it is certainly an aspect of self-actualization. You may think that you are an uncreative person. But it is more likely that you have been neglecting your creative self.

Note that it is not essential to upset the apple cart of your life and make self-actualization a full-time activity. You can be self-actualizing on a part-time basis. Many people say that they don't have time to become more self-actualizing. This is a rationalization. You need to *make* time for self-actualization by giving behaviors associated with it a high priority in your life.

Another important point is that you should not expect to arrive at a psychological destination where you say, "OK, that's it. I'm self-actualized. I'm complete." This is nonsense. Self-actualization is a *process*. You can grow and learn and enjoy the self-actualization process all of your life.

If you are self-actualizing, not only will the process help you to defeat depression, it will also open you up to *peak experiences*, spontaneous moments of joy and ecstasy. Maslow said that self-actualizing persons are more likely than others to have these peak experiences.

SEARCHING FOR MEANING

Actively Search for Meaning in Your Life. The existential psychiatrist Viktor Frankl said that each of us has an inborn *will to meaning*, a powerful impulse to discover values worth living for. Stated somewhat differently, the will to meaning is the need to make sense out of our lives and to live with a purpose. We don't want to believe that existence is absurd and chaotic. If we *do* think it is, this conviction contributes to depression. Indeed, the conviction that life has no meaning tends to induce *demoralization*, a completely hopeless state characterized by the spiritual wasteland described earlier.

How do you search for, and actually find, meaning in life? The answer is not as difficult as it may seem. Frankl, the philosopher Jean-Paul Sartre, and others who have thought deeply about the problem all seem to agree that meaning in life is associated with the discovery of values. *Values*, in the instance of the search for meaning, are associated with actions that have intrinsic worth. What are these actions? In general, they are given by your moral training and the ethical standards of your culture. Complete the following sentence spontaneously without too much thought or reflection: "I consider it worth doing to . . ."

Here is the way some counseling clients completed the sentence:

1. "I consider it worth doing to raise my children with love."
2. "I consider it worth doing to do a good job of repairing a customer's car."
3. "I consider it worth doing to give my parents some of my time and attention in their old age."
4. "I consider it worth doing to never cheat a friend."
5. "I consider it worth doing to respect my partner."
6. "I consider it worth doing to cook nutritious meals for my family."
7. "I consider it worth doing to tell my grandchildren a little about the way life was in the past."

As you can see, there is nothing unusual or remarkable about what most people consider worth doing. Values reside everywhere, close at hand. The problem, as Frankl notes, is that they often become invisible. They are *there*, but we don't see them because we have become blind to them. It's as if they are furniture in a dark room. However, a little reflection acts like a light switch. When the light of reason illuminates the room of the mind, we again perceive values that were there, like mental furniture, all of the time.

And Sartre emphasizes the importance of *action*. Once values are discovered, we discover meaning by actually *doing something*. Just thinking about values isn't enough. We need to turn good ideas into realities.

In most cases you will find that the discovery of values is really the *rediscovery* of values that you have neglected. So rediscover values, take action, and you will turn your search for meaning into the discovery of meaning.

ALIENATION

Reject the Alienated Life Position. A major contributing factor to existential depression is alienation. A state of *social alienation* exists when an individual feels disconnected from significant people in his or her life such as parents, a partner, children, or friends. The alienated person is an outsider. Think about the word *outside*. For example, for most of us a homeless person outside and alone on a winter night is a sad figure to behold. There is a natural feeling of concern for the well being of people who lack shelter.

People who are alienated may not lack physical shelter, but they lack emotional shelter. They are without the warmth of love and the comfort of meaningful human relationships. There is nothing clever, smart, or sophisticated about being alienated. It is important to feel that you *belong*.

Returning to Maslow, he spoke of *belongingness* needs as being important in the constellation of human needs. Like self-actualization, belongingness needs are also inborn. Individuals who think, "Who needs people? I sure don't. All I need is myself," are kidding themselves. Such thoughts need to be challenged with the cognitive tools presented earlier in chapter 5.

It is, of course, all right to either avoid or privately reject *some* other people. Not every person is someone you ought to like, love, or respect. On the other hand, if you cut yourself off from almost everyone, you are almost certainly making a big mistake. Again, challenge your own thinking on the subject. Dispute your own ideas. Look for the best in people. Be as forgiving as possible. Realize that sometimes people hurt you, yes. But it is frequently unintentional. It was a consequence of their behavior, but not its *aim*. Do your best to follow the old advice that it is best to forgive and forget.

Remember that you are being a "big" person largely for yourself. It isn't all altruism. If you are alienated, it will aggravate, as already indicated, an existential depression.

And you *do* want to avoid such depression for *your own welfare*.

MENTAL STIMULATION

Attend to Your Need for Mental Stimulation. Maslow and others have pointed out that an important need associated with the need for self-actualization is the need for mental stimulation. This need, also called the need for *cognitive stimulation*, is satisfied by providing the conscious mind with problems, tasks, and challenges. The understimulated mind finds the world and life to be lacking in color and interest. The properly stimulated mind finds the world to be a fascinating place of constant interest.

The understimulated mind is a bored mind. And a bored mind induces depression. Consequently, you want to make a distinct effort to seek out the kind of stimulation that your mind needs.

The stomach needs food in the form of proteins, fats, and carbohydrates. Similarly, the mind needs "food for thought" in the form of a steady flow of novel information. *Novel information* is information to the eyes, the ears, and the other senses that has some element of freshness or variety to it.

Below are a group of quotations obtained from various persons. These statements reveal various ways to meet the need for mental stimulation:

"Every day I work the crossword puzzle published in our newspaper."

"I read extensively—anything and everything I can get my hands on. It's all grist for my mental mill."

"As tough as it is, I do my own income tax preparation. I figure it keeps me on my toes."

"I like to go to swap meets and look for antiques. I like to haggle with the merchants and learn about the history of objects for sale."

"Stamp collecting is more than a hobby with me. I have learned a lot about U.S. history by collecting stamps associated with important events."

"I'm memorizing key lines from great poems. I find this interesting and inspirational."

"I build radio-controlled model airplanes. I enjoy trying to figure out how to correctly translate a set of plans and instructions into a functioning miniature machine."

Obviously there are hundreds of ways to meet your need for mental stimulation. Actively seek out ways that appeal to you and put them to work for yourself. It is an important aspect of your personal war against depression.

Here is a last and important point about mental stimulation. There is good evidence that a properly stimulated mind remains alert and functions well for more years than one that is neglected. There is even evidence hinting at the possibility that individuals who *use* their mental abilities are somewhat less likely to suffer in the long run from either Alzheimer's disease or senile dementia in general.

THE SELF AND THE SOCIAL WORLD

Bring the Private Self Into Better Agreement With the Social World. A very interesting psychological process that has been studied of late is called the *impostor phenomenon*. This condition tends to take place when ambition outreaches ability. For example, Langley D. works in an agency as a writer of advertising copy. He is only modestly talented and creative. He can do his job, but he has no great ability. However, he has an intense need for power, and dreams of attaining an important position in the agency. A few years pass. We look in on Langley now and find that he has become the director

of advertising, a position that requires substantial original thinking and creative ability. Langley has manipulated, pulled strings, and done favors to reach his present eminence.

It may seem that Langley is home free. But this is not the case. He has high blood pressure. He thinks he's getting an ulcer. *And he is depressed*. Why? Because he is suffering from the impostor phenomenon. He is in deep water and he is having a hard time swimming. In fact he feels that from a professional point of view he is drowning. He senses that his superiors have got his number and he is running the risk of being demoted or fired. He was clever enough to get the job he wanted. But he's not clever enough to do a good job of the job.

Langley is kicking himself for outreaching himself. And this kind of mental self-abuse is an important factor in existential depression.

The way to avoid being caught in the trap of the impostor phenomenon is given above. To repeat: *Bring the private self into better agreement with the social world*. Make a conscious decision to have a rational fit between what you *can* do and what you are *expected* to do. You will be much more emotionally comfortable if you will act on this suggestion. Too many people, particularly in organizations, are suffering needlessly from the impostor phenomenon.

LOCUS OF CONTROL

Accept the Reality of an Internal Locus of Control. Julian Rotter, a research psychologist, has discovered that whenever people act or react they tend to automatically attribute their action to a control factor. This control factor is perceived as either external or internal. If you believe that the course of your life is determined by chance, luck, them, the big shots, fate, the breaks, and so forth, then you perceive the locus of control as external. You do not perceive yourself primarily as a decision-making being, but as a puppet controlled by outside forces that pull your strings. This is, of course, a dismal perspective. Unfortunately, a psychological scale developed by Rotter suggests that a certain percentage of people *do* have such an outlook. And this outlook is associated with both learned helplessness and existential depression.

On the other hand, if you believe that the course of your life is determined by your will, your intelligence, and the decisions you make, then you perceive the locus of control to be internal. You *are* a fully functioning person in good spirits with self-confidence. You see yourself as the agent of our own growth and accomplishment. This point of view, make no mistake about it, is associated with mental health and freedom from depression. You want to do all that you can do to foster this outlook.

Note that there is no objective reality to internal versus external locus of control. There is, in a sense, no "truth" to either position. You can't prove the existence of a locus of control. Recall once again that you live in a psychological world of your own construction. Consequently, you can act *as if* a locus is real. And practical wisdom suggests that you should assert the personal reality of an internal locus of control.

Here are some positive affirmations that you can memorize that will reinforce an internal locus of control:

1. "I have a free will."
2. "I can and will make decisions in a confident manner."
3. "I believe in my own intelligence and creative powers."
4. "I am convinced that if I really want something and work toward getting it, I will eventually achieve my goal."
5. "Life is what you make it. It isn't something that happens to you."

The Last Word

One counseling client said, "There is nothing with greater gloom and doom than an existential depression. I ought to know. I have spent a few years of my life traveling through my own private Death Valley, a world of my own making. I've come to see that most of my suffering has been self-induced, a result of my outlook on life. So I've worked hard to reshape that outlook. And I can honestly say that most of my existential depression is gone."

Assert that you have the capacity to:

1. Become more self-actualizing.
2. Discover meaning in life.
3. Give your psychological world a new and better shape.

And you will find that your assertions become self-fulfilling prophecies. You don't have to live in an emotional wasteland.

Key Points to Remember

- An existential depression is present when an individual feels as if life contains nothing of value.
- An existential depression is not a *must* of modern life. It is a *risk* of modern life.
- Realize that you live in a psychological world.
- Become more self-actualizing. *Self-actualization* is the need to become the person you were meant to be. If you are self-actualizing, not only will the process help you defeat depression, it will also open you to *peak experiences*, spontaneous moments of joy and ecstasy.
- Actively search for meaning in your life. Meaning in life is associated with the discovery of values.
- Reject the alienated life position.
- Attend to your need for mental stimulation.
- Bring the private self into better agreement with the social world.
- Accept the reality of an internal locus of control.

7 IMPROVING PATTERNS OF COMMUNICATION: WHO IS MAKING YOU BLUE?

If, in a counseling session, a depressed person is asked, "Who is making you blue?" nine chances out of ten the psychotherapist will get a definite answer such as: "My husband," or "My wife," or "My boyfriend," or "My girlfriend," or "My mother," or "My father," or "My sister," or "My brother," or "My best friend." These people are called *significant others*, persons who play an important role in our emotional lives. These are the people we live and die for. These are the people we love. They are also the people who become the targets for our anger and hostility.

If a relationship with even one significant other is troubled, this condition can plunge you into a depression.

The psychiatrist Harry Stack Sullivan was one of the first researchers to note the importance of *interpersonal factors* in mental health. Sullivan's work inspired the psychiatrist Eric Berne, author of *Games People Play*, to develop a practical way of helping the average person understand self-defeating patterns of communication. More important, Berne's work provides useful ways to *improve* patterns of communication. These methods, specific interventions and strategies, will be brought forth with examples in this chapter.

Concepts in Transactional Analysis

In order to use and apply Berne's system, known as *transactional analysis*, in your daily life, it is important to begin by defining a few basic concepts. So consider this section a brief glossary. Practical applications will be presented in the next section.

Transactional analysis, or *TA*, is both a personality theory and a system that helps us understand and control patterns of communication between two or more persons. For convenience, examples will be limited to two persons at a time.

A *transactional stimulus* is a message sent by one person to a second person. A *transactional response* is a message sent back to the first person in response to that person's message. A *transaction* is an exchange of messages. Consequently, it takes both a stimulus and a response to make a complete transaction. Let's say a person says, "Hello. Good morning. How are you?" You are absorbed in thought and distracted. You fail to respond. There is no transaction, just a transactional stimulus.

A *stroke* is a unit of recognition. All transactions automatically convey strokes. Strokes can be *positive*, in which case they are taken as signs of love or affection. Strokes can also be *negative*, in which case they are taken as signs of hostility. An example of a positive stroke is a hug or a word of praise. An example of a negative stroke is an insult or a slap across the face.

Stroke hunger exists in all of us. It is the need for affection and the basic reason we engage in transactions. This, according to Berne, is the underlying motivation for human interactions. We don't outgrow our need for strokes any more than we outgrow our need for food. In the same way that food nurtures the human body, so do strokes nurture the human personality. Stroke hunger is so strong in human beings that they will often stay in self-defeating relationships that provide mainly negative strokes in preference to living in social isolation with no strokes at all. If a person either doesn't receive enough strokes or receives primarily negative strokes, he or she will tend to fall into a depression.

An *ego state* is just what it sounds like. It is a state your ego gets into. Think of your ego as a traffic signal with three lights. If the red light is lit, the orange and green are off. This is the *state* of the signal. If the orange light is lit, the red and the green are off. This is an alternative state of the signal. In the same way, you will see that your ego can be in one of three states. When you are "in" one state, you are "out of" the other two. Ego states tend to be turned "on" and "off" by the transactional stimuli others present to you.

The three ego states are the Parent, the Adult, and the Child. (It is a convention to capitalize ego states in transactional analysis in order to distinguish them from actual parents, adults, and children.) Ego states are not to be confused with living people. The ego states refer to the ways in which living people *act*.

The *Parent ego state* is commonly characterized by such traits as *overcontrolling*, *demanding*, *authoritarian*, *punitive*, and *idealistic*. It represents, so to speak, memory tapes your mind has made of ways in which you believe you were treated by your actual parents. These tapes operate in a semihypnotic fashion, and you often act without much reflection or thought in accordance with the dictates of your Parent ego state.

The *Adult ego state* is commonly characterized by such traits as *rational*, *logical*, *reality oriented*, and *reflective*. The Adult ego state has the power of foresight; it has the capacity to plan for the future. The Adult ego state is the one we must use to solve our personal prolems.

The *Child ego state* is commonly characterized by such traits as *impulsive*, *emotional*, *submissive*, and

self-pitying. It represents memory tapes your mind has made of the ways in which you acted and felt when you were an actual child. If a transactional stimulus turns on your Child ego state, you regress to a less mature stage of development. It is common to hear a first person say to a second person in an argument, "Oh, stop acting so childish."

Other concepts in transactional analysis will be defined as they naturally present themselves in the following discussion.

Using Transactional Analysis

Transactional analysis is a practical system that you can readily apply to your personal life. Its employment will improve your relationships with others in general. And such use will help you to defeat depression in particular.

Below you will find a set of practical strategies for putting transactional analysis to work.

RESPONDING FROM THE CHILD EGO STATE

Refuse to Respond from Your Child Ego State. Lorraine F. has been married for four years to Maurice. She tends to be a submissive person and he tends to be a dominating one. In the early stages of their relationship this resulted in a mutual attraction. She enjoyed being with a take-charge kind of guy, one who appeared to know what he wanted and what he was doing.Lorraine was comfortable with Maurice in the driver's seat of their relationship. However, Lorraine's submissive tendencies reinforced Maurice's dominating ones, and now the situation is getting out of hand.

Maurice is openly critical of many things that Lorraine does. He complains about her cooking, her housekeeping, and her taste in clothes. And how does Lorraine respond to Maurice's criticisms? Sometimes she withdraws and becomes uncommunicative. She pouts. She whines and complains. Sometimes she even *apologizes*. But in almost all cases she goes into her Child ego state when he turns on the emotional heat. And, of course, even though she has been married only four years, Lorraine is already suffering from depression.

It is a very, very common pattern in a marriage, or in any close relationship, for one person to dominate another one. However, it is essential to note that the submissive person unconsciously gives the dominating person power by responding repeatedly from the Child ego state.

When someone else tries to dominate you, this action pushes the button that activates the Child ego state. You will find it useful to say, "He or she is pushing my Child button. But I don't have to respond from my Child. I refuse to allow him or her to have this kind of control over me."

THE TEMPTATION TO EMPLOY THE PARENT EGO STATE

Resist the Temptation to Send Messages from Your Parent Ego State. The Parent ego state is a put-down artist. Maurice overuses his Parent ego state. He treats his wife like a child. You might think that someone who is capable of being top dog is the winner in a relationship. He, or she, is after all the "boss," right? No, it's not that simple. If you can maintain your dominance in a relationship, you will begin, unfortunately, to experience emotional isolation. And this will induce its own kind of depression. The other person will begin to withhold high-quality strokes, and you will experience a stroke hunger. Being overly bossy can definitely backfire, as indicated below.

THE PERSECUTOR AND THE VICTIM

Play Neither the Role of Persecutor nor the Role of Victim. In many self-defeating relationships one person plays the role of Persecutor and the other person plays the role of Victim. The *Persecutor* has sadistic tendencies and extracts pleasure from either the subtle or not-so-subtle psychological torture of the other person. Examples of persecution include hypercriticism, insults, cutting remarks, irrational demands, and hostile teasing. The Persecutor is acting out of the Parent ego state.

The *Victim* has masochistic tendencies and extracts a self-destructive pleasure from psychological pain. The hypercriticism, insults, and so forth of the other person act like little whips. Why does the Victim extract pleasure from pain? One reason, among others, is that the Victim

is carrying around a load of guilt and is convinced that he or she deserves to be punished. Sadistic behavior on the part of another person temporarily brings relief from guilt.

However, clinical observations suggest that the roles of Persecutor and Victim are not stable. They are just what they are called: *roles*. Consequently, roles are sometimes switched. The person who has been the Victim may suddenly turn and become the Persecutor. And the Persecutor becomes the Victim. Now the person who thought he or she held all the cards and was dominant begins to get used and abused, kicked around by a former Victim who has had enough.

Refuse to engage in a self-defeating relationship with someone else in which you play the role of either Persecutor or Victim. In the long run, playing these roles will intensify the depth of your depression.

ULTERIOR TRANSACTIONS

Avoid Ulterior Transactions. It is possible for a transaction to have two levels, the social and the psychological. The *social level* is what is actually said in words. For example, a first person may say to a second person, "I really love you," or, "You're my best friend," or, "I love that dress."

The *psychological level* is what is communicated by body language, facial expression, tone of voice, rate of speech, and so forth. A person who says, "I really love you" may communicate at the psychological level, "I'm bored with you," or, "The sex wasn't so hot," or, "I wish I was out of this relationship."

Ulterior transactions are dishonest. When the second person protests the psychological message, the first person acts hurt and innocent. "I *said* I love you! What more do you want?"

Sometimes ulterior transactions are said to be "crazy making." They are crazy making because they confuse and bewilder the mind, forcing the individual to sort out sense from nonsense. By the same token, ulterior transactions are also "depression making." They are depression making because they reduce the person's sense of worth, totally discounting authenticity in a human relationship. The receiver of an ulterior message is treated like a thing to be manipulated.

The person who sends ulterior messages will also be damaged because he or she is dehumanizing and devaluing a relationship. This too contributes toward depression. Both participants in ulterior transactions tend to pay a heavy emotional price.

YOUR LIFE POSITION

Reject the "I'm Not OK, You're OK" Life Position. According to transactional analysis, you can occupy one of four life positions. A *life position,* in this case, is the way in which you rank your own sense of worth in reference to others in general. The four basic life positions are: (1) I'm not OK, you're OK; (2) I'm OK, you're not OK; (3) I'm not OK, you're not OK; and (4) I'm OK, you're OK.

The person in the *I'm not OK, you're OK* position tends to have low self-esteem. (Note that the "I" is specific and refers to the individual self; the "you" is plural and refers to others in general.) Rhonda thinks that she is fat and that other women weigh less than she does. Suzanne believes that other people are smarter than she is. Logan thinks others are more creative than he is. Malcolm thinks that others are more relaxed and outgoing than he is.

The person in the *I'm OK, you're not OK* position tends to act in a superior and arrogant manner. The individual's self-esteem is distorted. An individual adopting this position seems to think that he or she is the gift of the gods to humankind. Mark believes that he has more talent than anyone else in his creative writing class. Lorne believes that he has, as he puts it, "A killer face and killer body that women can't resist." Georgina thinks that she is a woman of incredible beauty. Lenore believes that she is unbelievably charming.

The person in the *I'm not OK, you're not OK* position tends to not only have low self-esteem, but also thinks very little of the abilities and various attributes of other people. Lana thinks that she and everybody else in her English composition class are "stupid." Marilyn feels that she is an incompetent sales clerk; and she can't turn to the others for help because "they don't know anything either." Gable thinks that he is ugly; but the whole human race is seen as ugly and distorted. Ivan is unhappy and confused; but all psychotherapists are con artists and quacks. Consequently, they can't help him.

The person in the *I'm OK, you're OK* position tends to have high self-esteem and also has a high regard for others. Lucas thinks that he's good looking; and he thinks most people are good looking. Jason is ambitious and hardworking; he assumes that most people have similar traits. Kaitlin loves her children and is interested in child rearing; she assumes most mothers feel the same way. Lois sees herself as a competent student with high academic goals; she tends to attribute these positive qualities to others. The I'm OK, you're OK position is the only really healthy position of the four. The primary risk associated with it is that the individual may sometimes be a little too open and overly trusting.

The first three negative positions are maladaptive and nonfunctional. They create trouble in one's emotional life. In the extreme, they represent psychopathology.

The self-directed strategy in this section says to reject the I'm not OK, you're OK position because this is the principal one associated with depression. If you allow yourself to think of yourself as inferior to others, you will project this attitude into the social world. Then you *will* be treated as if you are an inferior being. And this will contribute heavily to your load of depression. As is emphasized subsequently, in a discussion of the Adult ego state, you *do* have a choice in the matter. You *do* have the power to reject an adverse life position.

THE LOSING SCRIPT

Reject the Losing Script. According to Berne, people often live by *life scripts*. A life script is a self-determined destiny. It was written by the Child ego state when the individual was an actual child, around the age of seven or eight. It is an immature decision that says, "This is the way that life will be for me." There are three fundamental scripts. These are (1) winning scripts, (2) nonwinning scripts, and (3) losing scripts. A *winning script* says, "I will achieve my primary goals in life. I will be successful and happy." People with a need for achievement that is both high and realistic will adopt a winning script.

A *nonwinning script* says, "I will be an also-ran. I'll never be in the front rank. I'll just be one of the crowd and muddle along. Life will be ho-hum and so-so for me." People who are ambivalent about themselves, who have some self-confidence, but not enough, are likely to adopt a nonwinning script.

A *losing script* says, "I will never achieve my primary goals in life. Many of my actions will be self-defeating. I will be unsuccessful and depressed. In the long run I'll get nowhere." People who lack self-confidence are likely to adopt the losing script. This, of course, is the primary script to avoid.

Thomas Hardy's classical novel *Tess of the D'Urbervilles* provides a clear example of a person who has adopted a losing script. Published in England a little more than one hundred years ago, it tells the story of a woman who engages in what seems to be a futile struggle against a malevolent fate. Tess is seduced at the age of sixteen by a man she doesn't love and has his child out of wedlock. The child dies. She eventually falls in love with another man, doesn't tell him about her past until her wedding night, and then is emotionally rejected by him. She works at dirty low-paying jobs for several years and eventually murders the man who seduced her. The murder becomes a kind of indirect suicide for Tess because she is eventually sentenced to die by hanging.

As suggested, a malevolent fate seems to chase her. But Berne's argument is that the fate of such a person is not objective. It is not made by the world. It is the person's script. And it was written not by the stars, but by the individual's own Child ego state. (Hardy, of course, does not use this kind of terminology.)

The story of Tess is presented here because of Hardy's remarkable insights into human nature. He was writing about forty years before Freud began publishing. It is clear from reading the novel that Tess is overly passive. She takes the harsh blows of life somewhat like a dumb animal. At no point does she seem to fully realize that she can use her intelligence and the power of her will to redirect the course of her life. In transactional analysis terms, she is playing the role of Victim to the hilt.

If you are living out a losing script, it is important to realize that you are obeying a decision made by your Child ego state when you were too little to really know what you were doing. Now that you are an actual adult you need to recognize that it *really is possible* to use your Adult ego state to reject a losing script. (More about this point later.)

GAME-PLAYING BEHAVIOR

Replace Game-Playing Behavior With Authenticity and Emotional Intimacy. A *game* in transactional analysis is a set of related ulterior transactions leading to a predictable negative outcome. When two people play this kind of game they are manipulating each other. There are cons and lies and other deceptions. The two individuals are treating each other more like things than like human beings. There is little or no genuine caring in a game. Each player is egotistical and self-absorbed. A game, in consequence, leads to emotional isolation. And this, in turn, is a significant factor in depression.

It doesn't take two people to stop a game. It only takes one. Imagine yourself playing a conventional game such as tennis. You are tired of the game and walk off of the court. The game is over.

Similarly, you can stop a self-defeating life game. A game is played out of either the Parent or the Child ego state. You can decide to function out of your Adult ego state. You can be authentic instead of overcontrolling or emotional. When you are authentic you are *real*. You give up masks and poses and pretensions. You become self-disclosing instead of self-concealing. You stop *using* the other person and cease to focus on what "I want." Instead, the focus becomes what "we need."

The payoff for authenticity is *emotional intimacy*. Emotional intimacy in a relationship is characterized by mutual understanding, respect, and genuine affection. It is a necessary aspect of every fully functioning relationship from a solid friendship to a durable marriage.

THE ADULT EGO STATE

Put Your Adult Ego State to Work. The key to implementing the strategies outlined in this chapter is the Adult ego state. This has been both implied and explicitly stated in much of what has been said. The Adult ego state is the problem-solving part of your personality. It alone, not the Parent or the Child, is oriented toward reality. It alone can help you break free from self-defeating personal relationships.

You have an Adult ego state. This is certain because you are conscious, can reason, can reflect, can evaluate, and have the natural capacity to will your own behavior. However, in many people the Adult ego state remains largely dormant, somewhat like a huge and powerful dynamo that is neither switched on nor plugged into a power source. You have to decide that you *can* switch on your Adult ego state, that you *can* plug it into the human power source that goes by various names such as inspiration or hope. Make this decision today, and you will begin to have a sense of freedom, a conviction that you are not trapped in a cycle of despair and depression.

Memorize these positive affirmations, and repeat them from time to time. They will help you put your Adult ego state to work; and they will keep it working:

1. "I have a free will. I have the power to make real choices and execute my decisions in the real world."
2. "I will be an authentic human being. I will be used and abused by no one, nor will I use and abuse anyone."

3. "I have the power to control my own behavior. I will allow no one to control me."
4. "I am an autonomous human being. I have the capacity for self-direction."
5. "I am a *proactive* being, not a reactive one. I can take charge of my own life."
6. "I trust my own intelligence and reasoning powers."
7. "I will be realistic and practical in my actions toward others, not impulsive and fantasy oriented."
8. "I am an adult and I have an Adult ego state. I am not a child; consequently I will not let my Child ego state make me the pawn of emotional reasoning."

The Last Word

Let's return to the question that was asked at the opening of this chapter: "Who is making you blue?" The odds are that you will be tempted to target some significant other person such as a spouse, a parent, a child, or a close friend as a major source of your depression.

However, another way of looking at matters is to suggest that, in a certain sense, *you* are making you blue. The only power that other people have over you is the power you give them.

To repeat, *the only power that other people have over you is the power that you give them*. Keep this thought in mind. By employing the power of your Adult ego state their influence over you is neutralized.

The strategies listed in this chapter, if actually applied, will help you to (1) become a more authentic person, (2) find emotional closeness in relationships that count, and (3) defeat depression.

Key Points to Remember

- If a relationship with even one significant other person is troubled, this condition can plunge you into a depression.
- *Transactional analysis,* or *TA*, developed by the psychiatrist Eric Berne, is both a personality theory and a system that helps us understand and control patterns of communication between two or more persons.
- Some key concepts used in transactional analysis are: (1) a transactional stimulus; (2) a transactional response; (3) transactions; (4) a stroke; (5) stroke hunger; (6) an ego state; (7) the Parent ego state; (8) the Adult ego state; and (9) the Child ego state.
- Refuse to respond from your Child ego state.
- Resist the temptation to send messages from your Parent ego state.
- Play neither the role of Persecutor nor the role of Victim.
- Avoid ulterior transactions.
- Reject the *I'm not OK, you're OK* life position.
- Reject the losing script.
- Replace game-playing behavior with authenticity and emotional intimacy.
- Put your Adult ego state to work.

8 DOCTORS OF THE SOUL: SEARCHING FOR MERLIN

Although there are many versions of the Arthurian legend, in the majority of them the figure of Merlin the magician looms large. He gives King Arthur wise counsel and helps him to grow as a person. In troubled times he is a staunch ally. He is more than a sage, he is a friend.

When we are troubled we yearn to find someone such as Merlin, someone who will help to guide us out of our personal emotional wilderness.

A psychotherapist, male or female, fits the image of a latter-day Merlin. He or she makes a real effort to help clients overcome personal problems. Although the Child ego state yearns for magic, the image of Merlin is, of course, too strong. A real psychotherapist may be able to help a depressed person, but the therapist should not be expected to be a miracle worker. In order for psychotherapy to be effective, the client must be an active participant in the process of psychotherapy. He or she must be willing to do a certain amount of psychological work. If you have unrealistic expectations for psychotherapy, you are likely to be disappointed and in turn become more, not less, depressed.

A *psychotherapist*, is, of course, a person who practices psychotherapy. And *psychotherapy* is defined as a kind of therapy designed to heal the wounded personality. The ancient meaning of the word *psyche* is "soul." And, so, in the broadest sense, psychotherapists are sometimes called "doctors of the soul." (The existential psychiatrist Viktor Frankl wrote a well-known book called *The Doctor and the Soul*.)

If you have made an honest effort to apply the self-directed coping strategies outlined in this book with limited results, you perhaps should seriously consider exploring the possibilities offered by contemporary psychotherapy. The aim of this chapter is to provide you with some basic information concerning kinds of psychotherapists as well as approaches to psychotherapy. This will make you a more well-informed consumer of this particular service.

Kinds of Psychotherapists

The principal persons who offer their services as psychotherapists are psychiatrists, clinical psychologists, and psychiatric social workers. A *psychiatrist* is a physician and holds an M.D. (doctor of medicine) degree. Psychiatrists are qualified to do psychotherapy and prescribe drugs. (More about drug therapy in chapter 9.)

A *clinical psychologist* has made an extensive study of human behavior and holds a Ph.D. (doctor of philosophy) degree. Psychologists are qualified to do psychotherapy and psychological testing. *Psychological testing* includes the employment of intelligence and personality tests, which are useful in making a diagnosis of mental health problems.

A *psychiatric social worker* has made an in-depth study of both individual and interpersonal psychology. A social worker capable of doing psychotherapy holds an M.S.W. (master's in social work) degree.

If you decide to go to a psychotherapist in private practice, make sure that he or she (1) holds one of the above degrees from an accredited institution and (2) has a state license to practice psychotherapy. Other reliable sources of psychotherapeutic services are hospitals and public mental health clinics funded by government agencies. Psychotherapists who work for a hospital or clinic need not hold an individual state license; instead, they work as supervised employees of legally authorized organizations.

Insurance plans will usually pay, depending on the plan, for psychotherapy up to specified limits. Public mental health clinics offer free services for some clients; a sliding scale, based on ability to pay, is provided for others.

General Characteristics of Psychotherapy

Although there are various approaches to psychotherapy, there are also general characteristics, features that all modes of therapy have in common. Let's identify a few of the more important features.

THE TALKING CURE

An informal designation for psychotherapy is the *talking cure*. Somewhere along the historical path, Freud's psychoanalysis was referred to with this label, and it has stuck. Indeed, it has been broadened beyond psychoanalysis to all approaches to psychotherapy. And, indeed, psychotherapy *is* a talking cure. It is a special kind of conversation between a therapist and a client designed to have a healing effect. The power of language is brought to bear, often with good results, on human problems.

HOPE

Psychotherapy is capable of *mobilizing hope*. People who seek psychotherapy are often more than anxious or depressed. Sometimes they are *demoralized*, meaning they have lost their capacity to hope. They will say such things as, "It's hopeless," or, "What's the use?" or, "I'm beyond help." Psychotherapy can help such individuals to begin to believe in themselves again. As one client said, "I realized after a few sessions that I was living in a psychological dungeon of my own making. And I began to grasp the fact that I was being handed keys that I could use to unlock the dungeon doors."

RAPPORT

It is generally recognized that in order for psychotherapy to be effective there must be *rapport* between the psychotherapist and the client. *Rapport* in French means "in close accord." The English usage is similar. When two people have rapport they are in emotional harmony. Informally, they "are on the same wavelength." If you decide to go to a therapist, you must get the feeling that the two of you "click" in some way. If this impression is absent, then it is unlikely that any actual therapy will take place.

Dennis G., a forty-seven-year-old man with adult children, was assigned a thirty-two-year-old female therapist in a mental health center. She was intelligent and well trained, but Dennis was unable to perceive her as his personal healer. He just couldn't convince himself that she had had the kind of life experiences that would contribute wisdom to his own personal problems. After three sessions, all of which seemed to be uphill battles, they both agreed that perhaps a different therapist would be better for him.

This does not mean that you cannot establish rapport with a person who is younger than you or who is not your own gender. But it does mean that whatever elements that will make for rapport in a particular case must be present in order for therapy to really take place.

GENUINE CARING

There must be *genuine caring* on the part of the therapist. Although a therapist is a paid professional, there is nothing cold blooded about psychotherapy. The therapist is not a mechanic who can fix the wounded personality independent of the therapist's inner feelings and attitude. This does not mean, of course, that the therapist should lose sleep over a client's problems.

The therapist who is in the grips of the social role of Rescuer will be overly idealistic and burn out. (It is a convention to capitalize the word *Rescuer* in order to distinguish the social role from an actual rescuer.) He or she will find it impossible to save every person from his or her own self-defeating tendencies. Nonetheless, the therapist must see psychotherapy as a high calling, as a meaningful vocation. And the therapist must sincerely give his or her best effort to every client.

FOCUS ON THE SELF

Psychotherapy *focuses on the self*. Its aim is to help you, the *individual*, make a better adjustment to the social world. Its aim is *not* to reshape that social world. Time is wasted in psychotherapy by belaboring all of the ways in which one is taken advantage of, used and abused by others, blocked from taking advantages of opportunities, and thrown aside by "them" or "the system."

Instead, energy is poured into what you the individual can actually *do* to improve your psychological and emotional situation. The idea is to make the best of whatever social world or life situation you find yourself in. In order to do this, you have to learn to dig into your own mine of psychological resources.

CHANGE AND GROWTH

Psychotherapy assumes that you can both *change and grow* as a person. And this assumption is made no matter what your age. We take for granted that the younger person can learn. But older persons can also derive great benefit from psychotherapy. The familiar saying, "You can't teach an old dog new tricks" is *not true* when applied to psychotherapy.

Many of our personal problems are caused by maladaptive habits. And these habits are not engraved in stone. They are encoded in a living brain and nervous system, and, consequently, are subject to modification.

Approaches to Psychotherapy

In the past, psychotherapists tended to belong to a particular school of psychotherapy such as psychoanalysis, behavior therapy, cognitive therapy, or humanistic therapy. Today the distinctions between the schools have become somewhat blurred; only a minority of therapists are willing to say that they practice one kind of psychotherapy exclusively.

Instead, the majority of contemporary psychotherapists subscribe to a *multimodal approach*. This is an approach made up of a combination of viewpoints, or individual approaches. The therapist tends to select and use those modalities that seem to best fit a given person's problem at various times during the therapeutic process. It is as if a skilled artisan was working with a kit of tools. At this moment he uses a saw. At a later moment he uses a drill. Still later he uses a screwdriver. The task to be accomplished elicits the tool to be used. Similarly, the skilled therapist, like the artisan, uses the "tool" or approach that will work best under a certain set of circumstances.

Below you will find the principal approaches used in modern psychotherapy. These approaches have informed prior chapters. Consequently, you can look upon some of what now follows as a brief summary of viewpoints that have already been discussed.

THE PSYCHODYNAMIC APPROACH

The psychodynamic approach is an outgrowth of Freud's pioneering work on psychotherapy. The majority of psychotherapists are not psychoanalysts, but they employ psychoanalytic, or psychodynamic approaches, in their work.

The central assumption of the psychodynamic approach is that human beings have an unconscious mental life. The unconscious domain is an unsettled realm of the personality containing primarily (1) repressed memories from early childhood, (2) forbidden sexual impulses, and (3) forbidden aggressive impulses.

Another important assumption of the psychodynamic approach is that the self is a battleground. A civil war often rages between the savage id and the civilized superego. This civil war, resulting in emotional conflicts, can play a significant role in depression.

When the psychodynamic approach is applied in therapy, the aim is to make the unconscious content accessible to the conscious mind. In this way the individual can gain greater understanding of emotional conflicts and bring chaotic emotions and impulses under rational control. The primary tool used to dig down into the unconscious is called *free association*. The client is encouraged to talk more or less at random about memories and feelings. And this often has a way of, little by little, bringing up unconscious material.

Another tool associated with the psychodynamic approach is *dream analysis*, in which an effort is made to explore the unconscious meanings of dreams.

THE BEHAVIORAL APPROACH

The behavioral approach to psychotherapy is an outgrowth of the research conducted by such individuals as Ivan Pavlov, John B. Watson, and B. F. Skinner. The central assumption of the behavioral approach is that maladaptive behavior is learned. According to this viewpoint, depression represents a kind of maladaptive habit. It is acquired through negative life experiences; and it is maintained by its psychological payoffs.

Applying the behavioral approach, a therapist will use such therapeutic interventions as behavior modification. *Behavior modification* aims at restructuring the way in which actions are psychologically rewarded. This can often bring about *extinction*, or unlearning, of a "bad" habit.

THE EXISTENTIAL-HUMANISTIC APPROACH

The central assumption of the existential-humanistic approach is that depression is caused by the way in which we relate to life itself. Two important ways in which we can fail ourselves is by not being self-actualizing or by not discovering meaning in life. Either failure can plunge the individual into an *existential vacuum*, a sense that life is empty of both joy and purpose.

Applying the existential-humanistic approach, a therapist will help a client (1) find ways to become the person he or she was meant to become and (2) discover the particular values that will make life meaningful.

THE INTERPERSONAL APPROACH

A central assumption of the interpersonal approach is that depression is often caused or aggravated by the way in which we relate to each other. If, for example, you play the role of Victim and allow others to manipulate you, to use you and abuse you, you will almost certainly be depressed.

Applying the interpersonal approach, a therapist will work with a client to develop more effective and mature ways to relate to other people.

The Last Word

All of the approaches described above are used in multimodal psychotherapy, the kind you are most likely to receive. True, one therapist may emphasize a particular approach more than another. But a licensed therapist who holds one of the degrees identified earlier in this chapter will be familiar with all of the approaches. And he or she will use the approach that best fits your problem at a given time in the course of therapy.

If you cannot help yourself out of depression, you are encouraged to seek the services of a qualified psychotherapist. But psychotherapy will not work for you if there is no rapport. If you and the therapist don't "click" with each other after a few sessions, don't feel guilty about looking for another therapist. This is the rational and intelligent thing to do.

If you *do* need a therapist, I hope you can find a person who can help you, through the applied wisdom of psychotherapy, to transform your life for the better.

Key Points to Remember

- *Psychotherapy* is defined as a kind of therapy designed to heal the wounded personality.
- The principal persons who offer their services as psychotherapists are psychiatrists, clinical psychologists, and psychiatric social workers.
- An informal designation for psychotherapy is the *talking cure*.
- Psychotherapy is capable of mobilizing hope.
- In order for psychotherapy to be effective there must be *rapport*, a mental and emotional accord, between the psychotherapist and the client.
- There must be genuine caring on the part of the therapist.
- Psychotherapy focuses on the self, on making a better adjustment to the social world.
- Psychotherapy assumes that you can both change and grow.
- The majority of psychotherapists subscribe to a *multimodal approach*, an approach made up of a combination of viewpoints.
- The central assumption of the psychodynamic approach is that human beings have an unconscious mental life.
- The central assumption of the behavioral approach is that maladaptive behavior is learned.

- The central assumption of the existential-humanistic approach is that depression is caused by the way in which we relate to life itself.
- The central assumption of the interpersonal approach is that depression is often caused or aggravated by the way in which we relate to each other.

9 ANTIDEPRESSANT MEDICATION: EXPLORING DRUG THERAPY AND OTHER BIOLOGICAL INTERVENTIONS

The idea that drugs can have an effect on personality and behavior is an old one. The ancient Romans used to say, *In vino veritas,* meaning, "In wine there is truth." In other words, the alcohol in wine brought out the repressed personality.

The novel *The Strange Case of Dr. Jekyll and Mr. Hyde* by Robert Louis Stevenson was published more than one hundred years ago in 1886. The beneficent Dr. Jekyll invents a drug that changes him into the evil Mr. Hyde. The name Mr. Hyde is intended to convey the idea of the "hidden self."

Modern-day drug therapy seeks to reverse the process described in Stevenson's novel. The aim is to use a drug to bring forth the better elements in one's personality. *Psychiatric drugs* are drugs prescribed to control such symptoms as delusions, anxiety, and depression.

Our focus in this chapter will be on drugs specifically used to treat depression. These drugs are prescribed on a fairly large scale. And you may find that a physician or a psychiatrist will, under certain conditions, recommend that you take one of these drugs.

Some General Considerations

Before specific drugs are identified, it will be prudent to become familiar with some general considerations concerning antidepressant medication.

1. If you find that self-help strategies and psychotherapy are inadequate to the task of coping with your depressive tendencies, drug therapy is a definite option.
2. Drugs are a treatment for depression, not a cure. In the same way that a person with diabetes does not expect insulin to cure the illness, a person suffering from depression can not expect a drug to permanently do away with emotional troubles.
3. Drug therapy can be combined effectively with both self-help strategies and psychotherapy in the battle against depression. Taking a drug does not mean you can expect the drug action to do all of the work while you rest on your psychological oars. Drugs, if used properly, help you to help yourself. And, eventually, you may be able to taper the dosage or eliminate the drug entirely with a psychiatrist's assistance.
4. Drugs sometimes have adverse side effects, and you should be aware of these. (More about side effects later.)

Kinds of Drugs

Drugs used to treat depression are called either *antidepressant drugs* or, simply, *antidepressants*. In general, they work by regulating the levels of certain neurotransmitters in the brain and nervous system. To repeat information also provided in chapter 2, *neurotransmitters* are chemical messengers that allow neurons to communicate with each other. *Neurons* are living cells that specialize in the transmission of information. They make sensation, perception, thought, and action possible.

An imbalance in neurotransmitters can be a significant causal factor in depression. When this is the case, the term *biochemical depression* is often used.

The choice of what specific drug to prescribe is determined by a given client's specific set of signs and symptoms. If the effect of one drug is disappointing, sometimes a prescription for a different drug is written.

TRICYCLIC AGENTS

The *tricyclic agents* have been the workhorses among the psychiatric drugs used to treat depression. They were developed in the 1960s, and have been in the forefront of what has often been called the "drug revolution" in psychiatry. The tricyclic agents work by regulating levels of the two key neurotransmitters involved in depression: norepinephrine and serotonin. Tricyclic agents are marketed under trade names such as Amoxapine, Doxepin, Elavil, Imipramine, and Tofranil.

MAO INHIBITORS

MAO inhibitors work by interfering with the action of a chemical in the nervous system called *monoamine oxidase*. The normal function of monoamine oxidase is to degrade excessive levels of neurotransmitters such as norepinephrine and serotonin. It is possible that in some people monoamine oxidase is "overactive." Consequently, too much norepinephrine and serotonin is destroyed, and the eventual psychological effect is a biochemical depression.

MAO inhibitors don't completely stop the effect of monoamine oxidase, but they slow it down. The net effect is to optimize the levels of norepinephrine and serotonin. Consequently, the end result obtained by taking a monoamine inhibitor is similar to the end result obtained by taking a tricyclic agent. MAO inhibitors are marketed under such trade names as Marplan, Nardil, and Parnate.

SPECIFIC AGENTS

A specific agent is a drug that works by targeting one neurotransmitter. Among the specific agents, one that has acquired quite a bit of recognition is *fluoxetine*. Fluoxetine works by inhibiting the re-uptake of serotonin by neurons. The net effect is to make more serotonin available to do its work as a chemical messenger. In other words, the aim of fluoxetine treatment is to raise serotonin to an optimal level for effective mental functioning. The primary trade name associated with fluoxetine is Prozac.

LITHIUM CARBONATE

Lithium carbonate is prescribed primarily to treat *bipolar disorder*, a kind of depression characterized by excessive mood swings alternating from mania to depression. Indeed, the older name for bipolar disorder was "manic-depressive illness." (See chapter 1.)

Lithium carbonate is a naturally occurring mineral salt and years ago was distributed as a mineral water. Lithium is marketed under such trade names as Eskalith and Lithotabs. Lithium was introduced into psychiatry as a possibly useful drug more than forty years ago. Although the pharmacological action of lithium is not as clearly understood as is the action of other psychiatric drugs, research evidence suggests that it, like other antidepressants, regulates the action of neurotransmitters.

Adverse Side Effects

Psychiatric drugs, like other prescription drugs, sometimes produce adverse side effects. These side effects range from rare to frequent; they vary greatly from individual to individual. Also, unwanted side effects can be mild or severe.

Side effects are due to the toxicity of a drug. Consequently, side effects must be taken seriously, and may provide a basis for changing dosage levels or discontinuing a drug. Below are of the adverse side effects sometimes associated with antidepressant medication.

1. Tricyclic agents may induce symptoms such as headaches, digestive upset, fatigue, sleep disturbances, and a craving for sweet foods.
2. A principal drawback of MAO inhibitors is that they can become quite toxic when taken in combination with foods containing *tyramine*, a chemical in the body that regulates blood pressure. When an MAO inhibitor is prescribed, the patient is supplied with a list of foods to avoid. If too many foods with tyramine are ingested, blood pressure can go up to a dangerous level. Foods to be avoided include certain kinds of cheese, fish, meat, and wine.
3. Fluoxetine, marketed as Prozac, is generally thought to be a drug of relatively low toxicity. Nonetheless, it can produce significant side effects in some individuals. Relatively common side effects include a reduction in appetite, sleep disturbances, and gastrointestinal complaints.
4. Common side effects associated with lithium carbonate include a tremor of the hands, a dry mouth feeling, shakiness, gastrointestinal complaints, a reduction in appetite, and a lowering in sexual desire. Lithium may in some cases have an adverse impact on thyroid and kidney functioning.

THE CONTROVERSY OVER DRUG THERAPY

Drug therapy has its critics and its advocates. Critics of drug therapy point to its adverse side effects and toxicity. They argue that drug therapy reduces the motivation to help oneself and to work in psychotherapy. A number of muckraking books have been published in an attempt to discredit drug therapy in psychiatry.

On the other hand, advocates of drug therapy point out that not all cases of depression respond well to psychotherapy. Advocates suggest that drug therapy can be combined effectively with self-help strategies and psychotherapy. Because of adverse side effects and toxicity, psychiatric drugs require a prescription and should be monitored by a physician.

The truth appears to reside somewhere between extreme viewpoints. It is certainly prudent to avoid taking a psychiatric drug if self-help strategies and psychotherapy are sufficient weapons in one's personal war against depression. However, if in an individual case, psychological interventions are inadequate, it may be necessary to turn to biological treatments such as drug therapy.

Electroconvulsive Therapy

Electroconvulsive therapy (ECT) requires the induction of a low-level current of electricity through the frontal lobes of the brain. If no muscle relaxant is given, the patient has a seizure that mimics the seizure associated with grand mal epilepsy. In contemporary treatment, a muscle relaxant is administered, and little or no overt muscle contraction results. Consequently, electroconvulsive therapy is not as hard on the skeletal system as it once was, particularly the spine.

About forty years ago ECT was a common treatment for schizophrenia and depression. Drug therapy has largely replaced ECT as a biological treatment. Nonetheless, there are times when ECT is prescribed. In the case of an individual suffering from a major depressive episode that does not appear to respond to any other treatment, ECT may be prescribed and administered. There is a consensus in the field of psychiatry that it is sometimes a useful treatment for intractable depression.

ECT seems to work in a manner that is similar to the action of some antidepressant drugs. It stimulates the nervous system to produce increased levels of the neurotransmitter norepinephrine.

Like all biological treatments, ECT should be used judiciously. Although a single treatment appears to do little central nervous system damage, a series of treatments may induce symptoms such as short-term memory impairment. This is because ECT appears to sometimes induce pinpoint bleeding in regions of the brain's cortex.

Premenstrual Syndrome

Premenstrual syndrome (PMS) may be a complicating factor in depression. The syndrome itself includes such symptoms as headaches, bloating and other digestive problems, irritability, fluid retention, dizziness, tender breasts, and depression. Premenstrual syndrome should not be confused with a milder and more common condition known as *premenstrual tension*. It is believed that about one-half of all women experience premenstrual tension from time to time. However, premenstrual syndrome is a clinical condition that affects about 1 percent or 2 percent of women. And it requires a physician's care in order to treat it effectively.

Treatment for PMS includes the prescription of nonsteroidal anti-inflammatory drugs, diuretics, and estrogen hormones. It is sometimes recommended that the patient take vitamin B_6 supplements and increase calcium intake. Frequently either antianxiety or antidepressant medication is also prescribed.

In the case of females, PMS should not be overlooked as a factor in depression.

The Last Word

Although this book emphasizes the value of psychological interventions in the form of self-help strategies or psychotherapy in the war against depression, we must not neglect the fact that drug therapy does have a proper place in that war. The enemy is depression. Any weapon that can help us to defeat it should receive serious consideration.

Key Points to Remember

- The idea that drugs can have an effect on personality and behavior is an old one.
- *Psychiatric drugs* are drugs prescribed to control such symptoms as delusions, anxiety, and depression.
- If you find that self-help strategies and psychotherapy are inadequate to the task of coping with your depressive tendencies, drug therapy is a definite option.
- Drugs used to treat depression are called either antidepressant drugs or, simply, antidepressants.
- The tricyclic agents have been the workhorses among the psychiatric drugs used to treat depression.
- MAO inhibitors work by interfering with the action of a chemical in the nervous system called monoamine oxidase.
- Fluoxetine is a specific agent. The primary trade name associated with fluoxetine is Prozac.

- *Lithium carbonate* is prescribed primarily to treat bipolar depression.
- Psychiatric drugs, like other prescription drugs, sometimes produce adverse side effects.
- Drug therapy has its critics and its advocates.
- Electroconvulsive therapy (ECT) is sometimes prescribed for individuals suffering from a major depressive episode.
- Premenstrual syndrome (PMS) may be a complicating factor in depression.

10 A SEVEN-STEP ANTIDEPRESSION PROGRAM

You have read all but this chapter of *Defeat Depression*. And you are convinced that there is much you can do to help yourself. But where do you start? With a number of options before you it is difficult to know which one to pick first.

You need a selection strategy in order to convert the book's suggestions into useful actions. Two such strategies are offered below: (1) the weakest link approach and (2) the seven-step antidepression program.

The Weakest Link Approach

Think of depression as a chain constructed out of maladaptive behavioral links. This chain binds you and restricts your freedom. But if you can break even one of its links, the whole chain begins to fall apart.

Consequently, look for the weakest links in the chain. Do this by flipping through the chapters and skimming the self-directed strategies. They are easy to find. All of them are identified with a distinctive typeface in, specifically, chapters 2 through 7. On index cards, jot down six or seven that have particular appeal to you, that you resist the least, that you believe you have some hope of putting into action. These particular suggestions point to several of the weakest links in your chain of depressive behavioral traits.

Carry the cards with you. Refer to them often and put the suggestions on them into action at appropriate times.

When the application of this first set of strategies has become habitual, it is time to make a second set of cards. Repeat the procedure described above.

The Seven-Step Antidepression Program

It is possible that you want to defeat depression in a more systematic, organized way. The purpose of this section is to lay out a blueprint for action.

The chapters in the book are arranged in such a way that they follow each other in a logical sequence. Each one is like a step on a staircase, a staircase leading upward out of the dungeon of depression. Consequently, you can make applications in a linear manner, following the given order of the chapters.

STEP 1

Turn to chapter 2, "The Psychobiology of Depression." If your depression has a biochemical basis, as it may, the suggestions in this chapter will help to give your key neurotransmitters a boost without drugs. Survey the suggestions listed under the heading "What You Can Do." Pick one that seems particularly important and put it to work. Continue in this manner for about one week. If you feel ready, then take Step 2.

STEP 2

Turn to chapter 3, "Rumblings from the Unconscious Mental World." If emotional conflicts play a significant role in your depression, as is likely, the suggestions in this chapter will help you acquire insight into them. The suggestions will also help you resolve some of your emotional conflicts.

Find the section headed "Coping with Emotional Conflicts." Select a strategy in accordance with the instructions given in Step 1. Follow the same procedure given in Step 1. After a week of application, go to Step 3.

STEP 3

Turn to chapter 4, "Overcoming Learned Helplessness." This chapter reveals how learned patterns of behavior aggravate depression. The chapter presents ways to either break or modify habits associated with depression.

Find the section headed "Habit Modification." Select a strategy in accordance with the procedure described in Step 1. After a week of application, go to Step 4.

STEP 4

Turn to chapter 5, "Depressing Thoughts." This chapter assumes that certain kinds of thought patterns called *automatic* and *irrational* induce a depressive mood. The chapter, based on principles of cognitive therapy, presents ways to challenge one's own negative thought processes.

Find the section headed "Coping with Your Own Thoughts." Select a strategy in accordance with the procedure described in Step 1. After a week of application, go to Step 5.

STEP 5

Turn to chapter 6, "Escaping from a Wasteland." This chapter examines the roots of existential depression, a depression arising from the way in which one relates to life itself. The chapter presents ways to overcome the demoralization that is likely to be associated with existential depression.

Find the section headed "Helping Yourself." Select a strategy in accordance with the procedure described in Step 1. After a week of application, go to Step 6.

STEP 6

Turn to chapter 7, "Improving Patterns of Communication." This chapter is based on the assumption that troubled relationships with significant other people in our lives often tend to induce a depressive mood. The chapter makes use of a practical approach to interpersonal relations known as *transactional analysis*.

Find the section headed "Using Transactional Analysis." Select a strategy in accordance with the procedure described in Step 1. After a week of application, go to Step 7.

STEP 7

You have earned a break. For about a week don't make any particular effort to apply the book's strategies. Allow yourself a vacation from your efforts.

About six weeks have passed since you started implementing the program. Perhaps the suggestions most useful to you are becoming second nature. You feel that you have climbed out of the dungeon of depression. If so, put this book aside. Return to it and put its ideas to work whenever you feel the necessity to do so.

On the other hand, you may, after a week's rest, want to repeat the program. If so, go back to Step 1. This time you might pick out alternative strategies, making fresh inroads into the problem of depression.

The Last Word

Depression is a complex emotional phenomenon comprised of both biological and psychological factors. In one person the biological factors may be the primary ones causing depression. In a second person the psychological factors may be the primary ones. In a third person the interplay of biological and psychological factors may be the dominant force inducing depression.

Consequently, there is no one best treatment for depression. The best treatment is the one that is best for the individual, the one that respects the person's uniqueness.

This is why it is helpful to study yourself and know yourself. Little by little you can become adept at coping with depression effectively. And this is true even if you seek psychotherapy or drug therapy. The more you understand about yourself, the better you will be able to cooperate with any treatment program undertaken.

You don't have to be a victim of depression. As I have said elsewhere in this book, you are *not* helpless. You need to know how to access your own power through the kind of practical strategies offered in the prior chapters. Accessing this power, you will find that you are really able to defeat depression.

Key Points to Remember

- This chapter presented two alternative approaches designed to help you defeat depression.

- The first alternative is the *weakest link approach*. Using this approach, you attack the problem of depression by selecting a group of six or seven suggestions that you believe you can put into immediate and effective action.

- The second alternative is systematic. It is the *seven-step antidepression program* outlined in this chapter.